Read On . . . Speculative Fiction for Teens

Recent Titles in Libraries Unlimited Read On Series
Barry Trott, Series Editor

Read On . . . Speculative Fiction for Teens

Reading Lists for Every Taste

Jamie Kallio

Read On Series
Barry Trott, Series Editor

LIBRARIES UNLIMITED

AN IMPRINT OF ABC-CLIO, LLC
Santa Barbara, California • Denver, Colorado • Oxford, England

Library of Congress Cataloging-in-Publication Data

Kallio, Jamie.
   Read on... speculative fiction for teens : reading lists for every taste / Jamie Kallio.
      pages cm.—(Read on series)
   Includes bibliographical references and index.
   ISBN 978-1-59884-653-9 (pbk.)—ISBN 978-1-61069-278-6 (ebook)
      1. Fantasy fiction, American—Bibliography.   2. Speculative fiction, American—Bibliography.   3. Young adult fiction, American—Bibliography.   4. Fantasy fiction, English—Bibliography.   5. Speculative fiction, English—Bibliography.   6. Young adult fiction, English—Bibliography.   7. Young adults' libraries—Book lists.
8. Fiction in libraries—United States.   9. Readers' advisory services—United States.   10. Teenagers—Books and reading—United States.   I. Title.   II. Title: Speculative fiction for teens.
   Z1231.F32K35   2012
   [PS374.F27]
   016.813'0876—dc23   2012014172

ISBN: 978-1-59884-653-9
EISBN: 978-1-61069-278-6

16   15   14   13   12   1   2   3   4   5

This book is also available on the World Wide Web as an eBook.
Visit www.abc-clio.com for details.

Libraries Unlimited
An Imprint of ABC-CLIO, LLC

ABC-CLIO, LLC
130 Cremona Drive, P.O. Box 1911
Santa Barbara, California 93116-1911

This book is printed on acid-free paper ∞

Manufactured in the United States of America

To Tara McGovern and Rebecca Pesavento, little sisters
who have taught me big things.

Contents

Chapter Three: Setting

Chapter Four: Mood

Chapter Five: Language

Series Foreword

Welcome to Libraries Unlimited's Read On series of fiction and nonfiction genre guides for readers' advisors and for readers. The Read On series introduces readers and those who work with them to new ways of looking at books, genres, and reading interests.

Over the past decade, readers' advisory services have become vital in public libraries. A quick glance at the schedule of any library conference at the state or national level will reveal a wealth of programs on various aspects of connecting readers to books they will enjoy. Working with unfamiliar genres or types of reading can be a challenge, particularly for those new to the field. Equally, readers may find it a bit overwhelming to look for books outside their favorite authors and preferred reading interests. The titles in the Read On series offer you a new way to approach reading:

- they introduce you to a broad sampling of materials available in a given genre;
- they offer you new directions to explore in a genre—through appeal features and unconventional topics;
- they help readers' advisors better understand and navigate genres with which they are less familiar; and
- they provide reading lists that you can use to create quick displays, include on your library websites and in the library newsletter, or to hand out to readers.

The lists in the Read On series are arranged in sections based on appeal characteristics—story, character, setting, and language (as described in Joyce Saricks's *Reader's Advisory Services in the Public Library,* 3rd ed., ALA Editions, 2005), with a fifth section on mood. These are hidden elements of a book that attract readers. Remember that a book can have multiple appeal factors; and sometimes readers are drawn to a particular book for several factors, while other times for only one. In the Read On lists, titles are placed according to their primary appeal characteristics, and then put into a list that reflects common reading interests. So if you are working with a reader who loves fantasy that features quests for magical objects or a reader who is interested in memoirs with a strong sense of place, you will be able to find a list of titles whose main appeal centers around this search. Each list indicates a title that is an especially good starting place for readers, an exemplar of that appeal characteristic.

Story is perhaps the most basic appeal characteristic. It relates to the plot of the book—what are the elements of the tale? Is the emphasis more on the people or the situations? Is the story action focused or more interior? Is it funny? Scary?

Many readers are drawn to the books they love by the characters. The character appeal reflects such aspects as whether there are lots of characters or only a single main character; are the characters easily recognizable types? Do the characters grow and change over the course of the story? What are the characters' occupations?

Setting covers a range of elements that might appeal to readers. What is the time period or geographic locale of the tale? How much does the author describe the surroundings of the story? Does the reader feel as though he or she is there, when reading the book? Are there special features such as the monastic location of Ellis Peters's Brother Cadfael mysteries or the small town setting of Jan Karon's Mitford series?

Although not traditionally considered appeal characteristic, mood is important to readers as well. It relates to how the author uses the tools of narrative—language, pacing, story, and character—to create a feeling for the work. Mood can be difficult to quantify because the reader brings his or her own feelings to the story as well. Mood really asks how does the book make the reader feel? Creepy? Refreshed? Joyful? Sad?

Finally, the language appeal brings together titles where the author's writing style draws the reader. This can be anything from a lyrical prose style with lots of flourishes to a spare use of language à la Hemingway. Humor, snappy dialog, wordplay, recipes, and other language elements all have the potential to attract readers.

Dig into these lists. Use them to find new titles and authors in a genre that you love, or as a guide to expand your knowledge of a new type of writing. Above all, read, enjoy, and remember—never apologize for your reading tastes!

Barry Trott
Series Editor

Acknowledgments

Many people played significant roles in the writing of this book, and for that I owe them thanks: my editor, Barbara Ittner, for her patience and spot-on suggestions; Barry Trott, series editor, for taking a chance on me; librarians Rick Roche and Heather Booth, for leading me in the right direction; librarian and book conservator Heidi Beazley, for all her paranormal fiction and graphic novels expertise; the writing community of Hamline University's MFAC program (love you guys); the Youth Services staff at both Morton Grove Public Library, Illinois, and Orland Park Public Library, Illinois, for their support and friendship and finally, to my family, especially my husband Kurt, who is always behind me one hundred percent of the way.

Introduction: YA, Here to Stay

Many of us who interact with teens—parents, teachers, librarians, coaches—have probably, at one time or another, thrown up our hands and despaired of ever getting them to read. And, quite honestly, why would today's sophisticated teens bother to read, what with media like YouTube, handheld video games, and cutting-edge smart phones to compete for their attention?

The truth? Teens read more than we think. According to a 2008 UNESCO (United Nations Educational, Scientific and Cultural Organisation) report on literacy rates, young adults are the most literate demographic, *worldwide*.[1]

The 21st century really is a golden age of young adult publishing, and guess what genres are the hottest? That's right, folks—fantasy and speculative fiction. In the words of Anita Silvey, former editor of *Horn Book* and a leading authority on books for young people, "Young adult literature [has] gained new passion, new focus, and new purpose."[2]

Being a staunch advocate for teen library services and a teen fantasy and spec lit fanatic myself, I fling out my arms in response to all this and cry, "YA is here to stay!"

Just Enough to Fill a (Bewitched) Teacup: A Totally Concise History of Teen Fantasy and Speculative Fiction

First, let us define our terms in their most basic sense: fantasy fiction creates a world where magic and mystical creatures exist, but this world can never be possible. Speculative fiction, on the other hand, looks outward at society, science, and the universe, and creates a world that *might* be possible. If we were to expand speculative fiction, we can also include paranormal (people, things, occurrences that lie outside the realm of normal—i.e. ghosts) and horror (terror, blood, guts—you get the picture). These definitions are not meant to be all-inclusive, but they do paint a general picture of what you'll find in each type, and all of these types are covered in this book.

Long before there even was a YA fiction market, teens read from the fantasy canon that was, for all intents and purposes, targeting adults as its audience. These massive, multivolumed sagas—by Terry Brooks, Robert Jordan, Marion

Zimmer Bradley, to name a few—can take someone years to get through, but for teens attracted to fantasy or spec lit, extreme page counts and complex story lines are not a deterring factor. My husband discovered the *Lord of the Rings* trilogy in sixth grade; an old boss of mine read Frank Herbert's *Dune* as a high school freshman; and I was reading the Anne Rice vampire novels at age 17.

There is an appeal to this genre that crosses all ages. Yes, it could be the escapism factor; really, don't we all, at times, want to leave behind our crummy job or that difficult calculus class for the more rewarding, lovely land of, say, Tolkien's Rivendell? The escapism theory, although true for many readers, is not the whole story. What draws many, many people to reading fantasy and speculative fiction is engagement with the characters—their coming of age, their morality, their rising out of a bad situation. For these readers, then, the otherworldly element is not their central concern.

Fantasy has been around as long as humans have been on earth. Every culture across the globe has folk tales, stories passed down from generation to generation that not only entertained, but cautioned, taught, or instilled a sense of justice in their listeners. There is a commentary on real life in fantasy and speculative fiction that rings loud and true, and this is a motivating factor for readers.

What makes teen fantasy and speculative fiction different, then? We could say page count, but then, there's that whole Harry Potter thing. J. K. Rowling is credited with getting a whole generation of not only children, but adults, reading. The immense popularity of the boy wizard not only changed the way kids read (many are no longer afraid of tackling a doorstopper-sized book), but it changed the publishing industry as well. Harry nicely filled the gap left between *The Baby-sitters Club* and *Gossip Girls,* and it showed those in the industry that kids were a serious and dedicated readership.

Enter *Twilight.* Stephanie Meyer tapped into a vein that solidified paranormal fiction for teens and brought the adults crossing over in hoards. Why? The appeal of following Harry Potter was to find out if this down-on-his-luck kid could find the courage to save not only his friends, but also himself. The intense love triangle between Bella Swan and Edward Cullen appealed to romance readers, but also thrilled them with high stakes and action. Again, readers crossed the lines because they wanted to follow the growth (or regression) of characters. Hot werewolves were just an added bonus.

Let's go back to that question: what makes teen fantasy and speculative fiction different from adult titles in the same genre? Teen fantasy and spec lit don't follow the rules. You can have a historical romance set in an alternative future with a dystopian setting, and it works—if only for its sheer audacity and vibrancy. Writers of this genre for teens are breaking away from the traditional fantasy tropes—male hero on a quest, damsel in distress, evil wizards, magical swords, ineffectual adults. While all those elements are still fair game in this new breed of teen fiction, we are now seeing warrior girl characters, boys who need saving, three-dimensional parents, and endings that are not always happy—thereby echoing a teen's real life.

Use Me Any Way You Want

There is no right way to use this book. It is intended for readers' advisory librarians, teachers, parents, teens, and anyone who has an interest in the genre. You may start at the beginning and work your way through, find a favorite author and pillage all his or her work, or you can find a certain list that grabs your attention and go from there. If you're a librarian, you can use the lists on your website, in your newsletter, or as handouts for teens who enjoy speculative fiction.

Here's a quick rundown on the organization: this book is divided by tastes. There are five chapters, each highlighting a particular area of interest, or appeal, and within the chapters are lists of titles grouped by a specific theme. Each title comes with a brief annotation, lending each list nicely to book talks or displays. You will find the author's name, title, series name, ISBN number, and pages for quick reference and easy buying; award-winning titles are clearly marked. Happily, most of the titles are now available as e-books; there is a select list of audiobooks as well.

Since teen fiction is constantly changing, the lists here are not exhaustive. You may also find that some of your old favorites are not included; that's because every effort was made to highlight novels from the last decade and also those that have been well-received and highly praised. Exceptions have been made for older titles of significant merit; otherwise, these parameters make this book relevant but also unique—it is the first of its kind to focus singularly on fantasy and spec lit for teens.

In short, there is something for everyone here, and I hope your reading gives you as much pleasure as does mine.

Symbols Used in Annotations

▶ Begin with this title, as it exemplifies the appeal factors of its chapter, as well as its theme.

🏆 This book won a major award in fantasy/scifi/spec lit and/or teen literature.

Notes

1. Hannah Withers and Lauren Ross. "The State of Publishing: Young People Are Reading More Than You." *Timothy McSweeney's Internet Tendency.* 8 February 2011. http://www.mcsweeneys.net/articles/young-people-are-reading-more-than-you

2. Anita Silvey. *500 Great Books for Teens.* (New York: Houghton Mifflin, 2006), Introduction, xii.

Chapter One

Story

Some of the world's most popular stories deal with the classic struggle of good versus evil. Why this theme resonates so deeply with people is anybody's guess. Famous psychologist Carl Jung proposed that humanity shares a collective unconscious, meaning that a shared common experience runs through the genes of all humanity, and we are therefore hardwired to engage in the good-versus-evil fight over and over again, for all time.

Collective unconsciousness aside, many readers of spec lit find the most important aspect is the story—the plot, the narrative, the anecdote; to be able to follow a series of related incidents from beginning to end, and in the process, learn something about themselves. Or perhaps in the most basic sense, these types of readers just want to be swept away. Use these lists to satiate your thirst for familiar themes or to try something new.

Take Me Away! Historical Fantasy

Love history? Love fantasy, too? Well, historical fantasy is the perfect storm for many readers, taking them away to another time and place—in more ways than one.

Bray, Libba
▶ *A Great and Terrible Beauty. Gemma Doyle Trilogy.* 2004, Delacorte Press, ISBN: 9780385732314, 403p.

Gemma Doyle, 16 and living in 19th-century India, experiences a terrifying vision of her mother's death. When her vision becomes reality, Gemma is sent back to England to attend the strict Spence Academy, where she is to learn how to be a proper young woman. Her visions continue, however, and soon she is able to enter the Realms, an addictive otherworld that she and her friends begin to crave.

Doyle, Marissa
Bewitching Season. Leland Sisters, 1. 2008, Henry Holt, ISBN: 9780805082517, 352p.

It's 1837 and 17-year-old twins Persephone and Penelope are starting their first London Season. Persy dreads the upcoming parties and balls, while her more outgoing sister, Pen, looks forward to them. They have been reared on magic by their beloved governess Ally, and when Ally is kidnapped, the girls set out to find her and foil a devious royal plot.

Hieber, Leanna Renee
Darker Still: A Novel of Magic Most Foul. 2011, Sourcebooks Fire, ISBN: 9781402260520, 320p.

In 1880 New York, young Natalie Stewart is entranced by a portrait of Lord Jonathon Denbury, rumored to have killed himself. Then Natalie discovers Jonathon's soul is trapped in the painting by demonic forces, and his possessed body is out committing horrific crimes. She realizes she will do anything to save him—even if that means entering the painting herself.

Owens, James A.
Here, There Be Dragons. Chronicles of the Imaginarium Geographica, 1. 2006, Simon & Schuster Books for Young Readers, ISBN: 9781416912279, 336p.

In 19th-century London, as World War I plays out, John's Oxford professor is mysteriously murdered and leaves behind a strange atlas, the Imaginarium Geographica, that supposedly contains maps to all the places that ever existed in myth and legend. Soon John and friends, Jack and Charles, find themselves traveling throughout time and place, on a quest to destroy the Winter King in hopes of ending the Great War.

Stanley, Diane
The Silver Bowl. 2011, Harper, ISBN: 9780061575433, 272p.

Molly is only seven when she is sent off to be a scullery maid at the castle, but she has a gift: she can see visions of the future. Years later, she discovers a curse that has been placed on a silver bowl, and suddenly she is charged with helping the royal family lift away the evil that has plagued them for years. First up—rescue the young prince from certain death.

Zink, Michelle
Prophecy of the Sisters. 2009, Little, Brown, ISBN: 9780316027427, 352p.

Alice and Lia are 16-year-old twins living in 19th-century New York. They are wealthy but have just buried their father, a tragedy that does not seem to affect Alice much. Then Lia's boyfriend, James, uncovers an ancient prophecy about two sisters who have the power to save or destroy the world. When an odd mark appears on Lia's skin, she realizes the prophecy is about herself and Alice—but which sister is evil and which is good?

(Bad) Politics, as Usual

It doesn't matter what world you're in, politics tends STET to be shady. These stories reveal lands that have succumbed to political intrigue or are right on the brink of political collapse. Luckily, there are always brave souls ready to fight for justice.

Bell, Hilari
▶ *Fall of a Kingdom. Farsala Trilogy, 1.* 2005, Simon Pulse, ISBN: 9780689854149, 422p.

Farsala is a prosperous and peaceful land, but an evil force is marching toward it—the Hrum, who have already conquered 28 other countries. The overconfident Farsala rulers mistakenly believe they can beat the Hrum. Three young friends, Jiaan, Soraya, and Kavi, see time's wheel turning, and they know Farsala will fall—unless they help.

Cashore, Kristin ♛
Fire. Graceling, Prequel. 2009, Dial Books, ISBN: 9780803734616, 461p.

Fire, who lives in a land called the Dells, is a human-shaped monster with stunning beauty and the ability to control minds. Her father is a corrupt advisor to the king and has used his own gifts for selfish purposes, so Fire vows to do only good with her ability. As the kingdom plunges into political upheaval, Fire is drawn into the conflict and has to make difficult decisions.

Dickinson, John
The Cup of the World. Cup of the World, 1. 2004, David Fickling Books, ISBN: 9780385750257, 432p.

Phaedra is 16 and refuses to marry any of her suitors unless it is the knight who's been visiting her dreams since she was a child. Finally, the knight appears in the flesh and Phaedra marries him instantly, though his family has a dark reputation.

Her decision causes war, and too late, Phaedra learns of her husband's chilling true nature. With all the odds against her, Phaedra must find the strength to stand up for what is right.

Fisher, Catherine ♛
The Oracle Betrayed. Oracle Prophecies, 1. 2004, Greenwillow Books, ISBN: 9780060571573, 341p.

Mirany is one of nine girls who serve the god-on-earth, Archon, but there are others in power who have evil intentions. Right before Archon dies, he tells Mirany to find the boy who is meant to take his place before the corrupt

Speaker seizes control. As Mirany sets out on her journey, she meets a motley crew of friends along the way and metamorphoses into a strong young woman.

Marchetta, Melina ♛
Finnikin of the Rock. 2010, Candlewick Press, ISBN: 9780763643614, 399p.

Finnikin was only 10 when the royal family of Lumatere was murdered, replaced by an imposter king, and a curse placed on the country that locked everyone else out. Now almost19, Finnikin is exiled and helps refugees. Then Finnikin meets Evanjalin, a girl who can enter others' dreams, and she reveals that the true heir to the throne is still alive—Balthazar—who can break the curse and regain the kingdom.

Marriott, Zoe
Daughter of the Flames. 2009, Candlewick Press, ISBN: 9780763637491, 368p.

Zira is 16 and lives in a temple in the land of Ruan, where she has been trained in martial arts as a warrior priestess. When her temple is attacked, she literally passes through fire and learns her true identity: she is really Zahira, the only surviving heir to the Ruan throne. After learning the truth, Zira rallies supporters and plans to take back her kingdom—but at what cost?

Pullman, Philip
Once Upon a Time in the North. His Dark Materials, Prequel. 2008, Alfred A. Knopf, ISBN: 9780375845109, 112p.

American aeronaut Lee Scoresby, and his rabbit daemon Hester, lands on the icy island of Novy Odense looking for work. The town is about to elect a new mayor, corrupt Ivan Poliakov, who wants to rid the place of all bears. Lee teams up with bear Iorke Byrnison to fight the corruption.

Let's Go, Already! Journey Stories

The hero's journey takes many forms and usually requires the help of loyal companions. Find grand adventures in the following stories and make some new friends along the way.

Abbott, Ellen Jensen
Watersmeet. 2009, Marshall Cavendish, ISBN: 9780761455363, 352p.

Fourteen-year-old Absina is an outcast in Vranille because of her dark coloring. When a new leader incites the people to murder all outcasts, Absina loses her mother and flees. She decides to find the father she's never known in a place called Watersmeet and sets out on her travels with Haret, a dwarf, at her side.

Alexander, Lloyd
The Rope Trick. 2002, Dutton Children's Books, ISBN: 9780525470205, 256p.

Lidi is a young magician determined to be the greatest of all, but to do this she must first learn the celebrated rope trick. The only person who knows how to perform the trick is the legendary (and slippery) master magician Ferramondo. Lidi assembles a troupe of friends and sets out to find Ferramondo, and romance blooms along the way.

Chabon, Michael 🏆
Summerland. 2002, Miramax Books/ Hyperion Books for Children, ISBN: 0786808772, 550p.

Ethan Feld is the worst baseball player in the history of Little League. Then his inventor dad is kidnapped by evil Coyote, and he is recruited by Ringfinger Brown, an old-timer from the Negro baseball leagues, to save the world! To do this, Ethan and his friends go on a road trip, pop in and out of universes, including Summerland, and Ethan has to play the baseball games of his life.

Dickinson, Peter 🏆
The Ropemaker. 2001, Delacorte Press, ISBN: 978038572915, 375p.

Tilja's family has been part of the magical forces that protect their valley for generations. When the magic starts to fail, Tilja, her friend Tahl, and their grandparents travel across unfamiliar and evil territory in search of the one man who might restore their safety.

Gaiman, Neil
▶ *Stardust.* 2006, Harper Perennial, ISBN: 9780061142024, 250p.

In the town of Wall (named for the granite wall running to its east), Tristan Thorn has a crush on frosty Victoria Forester. Victoria is only toying with Tristan, and when they watch a star fall from the night sky, she teases that she will marry him if he can retrieve the star for her. Determined to win her hand, Tristan finds a gap in the wall, climbs into an unforgettable land, and searches for the star—which turns out to be another kind of miracle.

Halpern, Jake
Dormia. 2009, Houghton Mifflin, ISBN: 9780547076652, 506p.

Twelve-year-old Alfonso has amazing skill at fighting and sports; he can do it all while asleep. When Uncle Hill appears, he reveals that Alfonso is from Dormia, a kingdom hidden in the Ural Mountains and whose inhabitants are all wakeful sleepers. Now Alfonso learns that the strange plant he has been tending is actually a Dormian bloom and must be returned to the kingdom of Dormia in order to save it.

Pierce, Tamora
The Will of the Empress. 2005, Scholastic, ISBN: 9780439441728, 550p.

Sixteen-year-old Sandry and her three friends, Tris, Briar, and Daja, were once as close as siblings, with a telepathic connection and magical abilities. But as all four have gone separate ways, their connection has weakened. When

Sandry must travel to her lands in order to keep her cousin, the empress, from usurping them, her three long-lost friends accompany her.

Tolkien, J.R.R.
The Hobbit, or There and Back Again. Lord of the Rings. 2001, Houghton Mifflin, ISBN: 0618162216, 330p.

Bilbo Baggins is a Hobbit enjoying a pleasant life in the Shire until he is visited by wizard Gandalf the Grey. Gandalf needs a companion for an adventure, and though Bilbo is unwilling, he suddenly finds himself traveling with the wizard and a band of dwarves, intent on reclaiming stolen treasure from the dragon Smaug. Along the way, Bilbo wins and brings home a ring.

Ye Gods! Stories of Mythical Proportions

Remember what a snooze fest that unit on mythology was in school? Had a hard time keeping all the Greek, Roman, and Norse gods straight? Well, never fear! The following titles keep it all straight for you, and they're anything but boring.

Abouzeid, Chris
Anatopsis. 2006, Dutton Children's Books, ISBN: 0525475834, 336p.

Anatopsis is soon to be 13 and her mother, Queen Solomon, wants Ana to follow in her witchcraft ways. To this end, Mr. Pound is hired to tutor Ana in preparation of her Bacchanalian exams, but strange things start to happen. Soon Ana and her friends Barnaby and Clarissa realize that Mr. Pound is a demigod intent on destroying the mortal world, all with a magical artifact and the answer to a puzzling riddle.

Farmer, Nancy ♈
Sea of Trolls. Sea of Trolls Trilogy, 1. 2004, Atheneum Books for Young Readers, ISBN: 9780689867446, 459p.

The Bard trained 11-year-old Jack in magic and Norse history before Jack and his little sister, Lucy, are kidnapped by Viking Berserkers. He is brought before King Ivar the Boneless and offends his wife, the half-troll Queen Frith. The queen sends Jack on a quest to Troll country, where he must find her a beauty elixir, or else Lucy will be sacrificed.

Harris, Joanne
Runemarks. 2008, Alfred A. Knopf, ISBN: 9780375844447, 526p.

Maddy Smith lives in a society that sprang up 500 years after Ragnarok, the Norse version of the Apocalypse. Magic is now forbidden, but this doesn't stop the ancient rune mark from appearing on Maddy's hand. Her mentor, a wanderer named One-Eye, instructs her in magic and teaches her the legend of Vanir and Aesir. As Maddy's powers strengthen, she awakes old magic and learns that the legends are actually true—and she has become a major player in the war between the rising gods.

Napoli, Donna Jo
The Great God Pan. 2003, Wendy Lamb Books, ISBN: 0385327773, 149p.

Pan is a half-man, half-goat demigod, and he has always been happy frolicking in the woods, partaking in physical pleasures, and playing his reed pipes. When he happens on Iphigenia, a girl raised by Agamemnon and Queen Clytemnestra, he falls instantly in love. Everything changes as Pan begins to question family, belonging, and sacrifice.

Riordan, Rick ♛
▶ *The Lightning Thief. Percy Jackson and the Olympians, 1.* 2006, Miramax, ISBN: 9780786838653, 377p.

Percy Jackson always knew he was different, what with his dyslexia and attention deficit disorder, but he never expected to be the son of the Greek sea god, Poseidon. After a winged monster tries to kill him in the Metropolitan Museum of Art, Percy is shipped off to Camp Half Blood, a magically protected place where demigods learn to battle. Things get worse for Percy when Zeus accuses him of stealing his lightning bolt, leading Percy and his friends on a quest to find the real thief.

Ursu, Anne
The Shadow Thieves. The Cronus Chronicles, 1. 2006, Atheneum Books for Young Readers, ISBN: 9781416905875, 432p.

Unremarkable Charlotte likes to keep the status quo, but all that changes when her British cousin Zee visits. All of Zee's friends have become terribly ill back in England, and he finds the same thing is happening to his new friends in America. Charlotte and Zee soon learn that Philonecron, born in the underworld of Hades, plans to reanimate the dead and take over Hades's throne, and he's using Zee to do just that.

Whitman, Emily
Radiant Darkness. 2009, HarperCollins, ISBN: 9780061780356, 274 p.

Persephone is innocent, living in paradise with her goddess mother, Demeter, and bored. The thought of spending eternity in her mother's realm is too much, and when a mysterious young man named Hades enters the picture, she readily runs off to the Underworld with him. Demeter threatens to destroy earth if Persephone doesn't return, so she must make a choice—stay with Hades for love or save the world.

Holy Smokes! Dragons

Dragons might just be the coolest pets in the universe—if they're friendly. If not, well, let's just say you might want to invest in a few extra smoke detectors.

Day, Jessica George
Dragon Slippers. 2007, Bloomsbury Children's Books, ISBN: 9781599900575, 336p.

After Creel is orphaned, her aunt takes her in and hatches a scheme: Creel will go to the local dragon, and hopefully a rich knight will come to her aid, thereby saving the relatives from poverty. The dragon ends up being a gentle, shoe-collecting soul who doesn't want to fight a knight and encourages Creel to take a pair of blue slippers. Little does Creel know the power behind the slippers, and when they fall into the wrong hands, she must find a way to save her dragon friend.

Goodman, Alison ♛
Eon: Dragoneye Reborn. 2008, Viking Juvenile, ISBN: 0670062278, 544 p.

Women are forbidden to study dragon magic, so 16-year-old, crippled Eon disguises herself as a boy to train. The chances of a dragon choosing a female apprentice are slim, yet Eon is surprised when the Mirror Dragon selects her. The Mirror Dragon has been absent for 500 years, and Eon's new mentor thrusts her into the center of political intrigue.

Jordan, Sherryl ♛
The Hunting of the Last Dragon. 2002, HarperCollins, ISBN: 9780060289034, 186p.

In an alternative 14th-century England, Jude is an illiterate peasant with a fantastic tale to tell. He tells his story to Brother Benedict, in the hopes of recording his adventures in which he saved a foot-bound Chinese woman, an ancient witch, and a destiny that involves killing an evil dragon.

Knudsen, Michelle
▶ *The Dragon of Trelian.* 2009, Candlewick Press, ISBN: 9780763634551, 407p.

Calen is a wizard's apprentice and is frustrated with his life. Unexpectedly he meets Princess Meglynne and the two become fast friends. Meg shares her secret with Calen—she has discovered a baby dragon and has bonded deeply with the creature. As the friends deal with the complications behind this secret, Calen learns more about magic and his own abilities—which come in handy when the royal family is threatened.

Paolini, Christopher
Eragon. Inheritance Cycle, 1. 2003, Alfred A. Knopf, ISBN: 9780375826689, 528p.

Eragon is a 15-year-old farm boy who discovers a blue egg in the forest. The egg hatches a sapphire-blue dragon, and she and Eragon instantly bond. Eragon then learns that he is the first new Dragon Rider to emerge in 100 years. Suddenly he must train with the dragon (Saphira), learn magic and martial arts, and avoid the evil King Galbatroix, who wants this latest Dragon Rider to serve as his minion.

Stroud, Jonathan
Buried Fire. 2004, Miramax, ISBN: 9780786851942, 336p.

Michael MacIntyre falls asleep on a hill that is a burial for an ancient, evil dragon. The curse that holds the dragon is a Celtic cross, and when that cross is unearthed by four villagers, the dragon's powers begin to awaken. When Michael is possessed by the dragon, his siblings, Stephen and Sarah, try to stop the spell before it completely consumes him.

Look, Ma, I Can Fly!…and Other Experiments

Humans are curious beings. We're always playing with the rules, trying to push the known boundaries as far as we can. Too often, though, we end up pushing off the cliff of those boundaries, leaving behind messy, horrific experiments.

Bodeen, S. A.
The Gardener. 2010, Feiwel and Friends, ISBN: 9780312370169, 233p.

High school sophomore Mason dreams of going to college and becoming a biologist. In order to do that, he has to apply for an internship at TroDyn, the local bioengineering firm. TroDyn also owns a nursing home for catatonic teenagers, where Mason's mom works. When Mason visits, an amazingly beautiful girl wakes from her coma and begs Mason to help her escape. Mason makes a shocking discovery—the girl has plantlike qualities, so she can photosynthesize her own food.

Clements, Andrew ♛
Things Not Seen. 2002, Philomel Books, ISBN: 0399236260, 251p.

One morning after taking a shower, 15-year-old Bobby Phillips looks in the mirror and doesn't see himself. He is gone—invisible. His parents tell him to stay inside while his physicist father searches for an explanation, but tired of being unseen, Bobby ventures out swaddled in layers of clothes. He visits the library and meets Alicia, a blind girl, to whom he confides his secret. Together they try to solve Bobby's problem as the clock ticks—authorities want to know why he hasn't shown up for school, and his parents are suspected of murdering him.

Dashner, James ♛
The Maze Runner. 2009, Delacorte Press, ISBN: 9780385737944, 384p.

Sixteen-year-old Thomas wakes up with no memory in the middle of a maze. There are other teens in the maze, too, and no one remembers how they got there. In hopes of escape, they send out runners each day to search for a way out of the constantly changing maze. There are also bizarre monsters called Grievers stalking them. In the midst of it all, Thomas struggles with some hazy memories.

Haddix, Margaret Peterson
Turnabout. 2000, Simon & Schuster Books for Young Readers, ISBN: 0689821875, 223p.

In the year 2000, Melly and Anny Beth are old and living in a nursing home. When they are offered the chance to participate in a top secret unaging experiment, they jump. When the reader meets them, it is 2085, and Melly is now 16, Anny Beth is 18, and as they age backwards, they worry about who will care for them as they turn back into children, then babies, and finally, die.

Halam, Ann ♛
Dr. Franklin's Island. 2002, Wendy Lamb Books, ISBN: 038573008x, 245p.

Semirah is one of 50 science students traveling by plane to work with conservationists in Ecuador. When the place crashes on a remote island, only three teens survive—Semirah, Miranda, and Arnie. As they struggle to survive and to locate help, they discover the island's other inhabitants—the crazed Dr. Franklin, who is trying to create a new breed of human that can mutate to animals. When the teens are captured, they become subjects in Dr. Franklin's horrific experiment.

Patterson, James
▶ *The Angel Experiment. Maximum Ride, 1.* 2005, Little, Brown, ISBN: 9780316067959, 422p.

Fourteen-year-old Max (short for Maximum Ride) and her flock have escaped the school that grafted avian DNA onto their genes, which allows them to fly. The school kept the birdkids locked in cages and tortured them in the name of science, and they created other things—the Erasers, vicious half-men, half-wolves who are on the birdkids' trail. When the youngest, Angel, is captured and brought back to the school, Max and the gang set out on a rescue mission, determined to save her—and to learn the truth about their origins.

Reichs, Kathy
Virals. 2010, Razorbill, ISBN: 9781595143426, 454p.

Tory Brennan, age 14, has lost her mother and now lives with her marine-biologist father on an island off the South Carolina coast. When she and her friends explore a seemingly deserted lab complex, they find a caged half-wolf, half-dog that has been infected with parvovirus. To save the dog from being tested on, Tory rescues it, knowing that humans cannot catch parvo. Soon after treating the dog, however, Tory and her friends begin to exhibit strange symptoms that magnify their senses.

Westerfeld, Scott
Specials. Uglies, 3. 2006, Simon Pulse, ISBN: 0689865406, 372p.

Tally Youngblood, aged 16, has spent a lot of time fighting against Dr. Cable and her corrupt government that brainwashes its citizens with surgeries that make everyone pretty. But Tally is captured and programmed to be a highly dangerous government agent—a Special—charged with wiping out the New Smoke, a rebel colony, where Tally's once-boyfriend Zane lives. This is the third installment of the *Uglies* series—be sure to start with *Uglies*.

Fantasia: Stories of Music and Magic

Sometimes listening to or creating music can utterly enchant you with its melodious spell and carry you off to another world. These stories offer up the magical power of music—in a literal sense.

Stoffels, Karlijin
Heartsinger. 2009, Arthur A. Levine Books, ISBN: 9780545069298, 134p.

Mee is renowned for his beautiful voice; he is a singer of sorrows, and people call on him to sing the pain out their hearts. On the other side of the land, another glorious singer, Mitou, has heard of Mee and begins to journey toward him, feeling they are destined to meet. What might happen when a singer of sorrow collides with a singer of joy?

Taylor, Greg
The Girl Who Became a Beatle. 2011, Feiwel & Friends, ISBN: 9780312652593, 288p.

Sixteen-year-old Regina's band, the Caverns, has just broken up. In despair she wishes they were still together and as famous as the Beatles. As luck would have it, a fairy godmother grants this wish, and Regina wakes up into a world where the Caverns are the musical gods, and the Beatles have never existed. At first Regina likes her new life, but she can't stop her longing for her real world.

Thompson, Kate ♛
The New Policeman. 2005, Bodley Head, ISBN: 9780370328232, 279p.

Irish teen J. J. Liddy takes his mother's request for extra time seriously. A musician, J. J. discovers that wild, raucous music is the bridge between the mortal world and Tir na Nog, the land of the fairies, where he might be able to steal some time. But once in this land of eternal youth, J. J. uncovers secrets—about his own family, the identity of his town's new policeman, and that there is a time leak between worlds.

Watts, Leander
Beautiful City of the Dead. 2006, Houghton Mifflin 2006, ISBN: 9780618594436, 256p.

Zee plays bass and scribbles lyrics down in a notebook. She is thrilled when Relly asks her to join Scorpio Bone, his heavy metal band. The musicians bond instantly and create a screeching, intense sort of sound that seems otherworldly. As strange happenings abound, Zee realizes that the band is otherworldly—each of the teens develop supernatural powers and find themselves embroiled in a war between the gods.

Westerfeld, Scott
The Last Days. 2006, Razorbill, ISBN: 9781595140623, 286p.

With New York in the grasp of an ancient evil, and humans falling to the Peeps plague, Moz and his friend Zahler roam the cracking city streets in search of other musicians. Enter Pearl, Alana Ray, and Minerva—all a little off-kilter—and the band is formed. As Moz and his friends create an intense sound track, they realize they all just might have the power to defeat the evil forces.

Yolen, Jane and Adam Stemple ♛
▶ *Pay the Piper. Rock n' Roll Fairy Tales, 1.* 2005, Starscape, ISBN: 9780765311580, 176p.

All Callie wanted was to go to a concert so she could write a review for her school paper. The leader of the band, Brass Rat, is really an exiled Faery Prince, who must offer up silver, gold, or souls every seven years. When Halloween rolls around, the Piper decides to lure away the trick-or-treaters—including Callie's brother.

Once Upon a Twist: Fairy Tales Old and Retold

Fairy tales and legends have been around as long as there have been people on earth. Modern fairy tales take your happy little children's stories and spice them up with vivid characters, magic, and sometimes blood and guts. But only sometimes.

Bunce, Elizabeth C. ♛
A Curse Dark as Gold. 2008, Arthur A. Levine Books, ISBN: 978043989576, 395p.

In this spin on Rumpelstiltskin, 17-year-old Charlotte is left to run the family's wool mill after her father's death. No matter what she does, however, the mill keeps running into bad luck, almost as if it were cursed. When a strange little man comes along and offers to spin straw into gold, Charlotte is tempted to take him up on it—but at what price?

Finn, Alex
Beastly. 2007, HarperTeen, ISBN: 9780060874162, 304p.

Kyle is a jerk, the rich, good-looking kid everybody envies. When he literally turns into a beast, his father locks him away in a Manhattan sky rise, where Kyle spends his days languishing away in depression. To return to his human form, he must find true love, but which beauty would love him now?

George, Jessica Day ♛
Princess of the Midnight Ball. 2009, Bloomsbury, ISBN: 9781599903224, 280p.

Because of a bargain their dead mother made with the evil King Under Stone, princess Rose and her 11 sisters must dance every night with the king's sons until their slippers are worn to shreds. A young soldier named Galen finds work as the castle gardener, falls in love with Rose, and uncovers the mystery behind their exhaustion. Determined to help Rose, Galen must somehow break the curse.

Hale, Shannon
The Goose Girl. Books of Bayern, 1. 2003, Bloomsbury, ISBN: 9781582349909, 383p.

Princess Ani can speak to animals, but this ability does not stop her guards and lady-in-waiting from betraying her. Exiled from her land, Ani disguises herself as a goose girl until she can reveal her true identity and reclaim her throne.

Marillier, Juliet 🏆
▶ *Wildwood Dancing.* 2007, Alfred A. Knopf, ISBN: 9780375844744, 407p.

Jena and her four sisters live in a castle called Piscul Draculi, in Transylvania. Jena and her pet frog love her family and home, and they especially love full moon nights, when they pass through a portal to an enchanted fairy realm. Their way of life is threatened, however, when their father takes ill and their powerful cousin Cezar takes charge. Complicating all is Jena's oldest sister's romance with a dangerous boy from the other realm.

Marriott, Zoe
The Swan Kingdom. 2009, Candlewick, ISBN: 9780763642938, 272p.

Alexandra is born with certain powers but she doesn't know how to use them yet, a fact that comes to light when her mother is killed and she can't do anything to help. When she objects to her father's sudden new bride, the king banishes her and turns her brothers into swans. Only while she is in exile does Alexandra learn about her abilities, and then she decides to take matters into her own hands.

Pattou, Edith 🏆
East. 2005, Magic Carpet Books, ISBN: 9780152052218, 507p.

Don't you hate it when parents lie? Rose is a North-born baby, which, in her superstitious Norway village, means that she will grow up to be a wild, uncontrollable person full of wanderlust. To keep this fate from occurring, Rose's mother lied and said she was a child of the East. But when a great white bear shows up, Rose's destiny can no longer be denied.

Dead Zone: Stories from beyond the Grave

Have you ever felt like someone was trying to send you a message—from the afterlife? Better yet, have you ever thought about contacting your loved ones—after you've passed on? Nobody really knows what happens after death, but these stories do a pretty good job of answering the question, "What if?"

Colfer, Eoin

The Wish List. 2003, Miramax Books/Hyperion Books for Children, ISBN: 9780786818631, 252p.

Forced into a life of crime by her cruel stepfather, 14-year-old Meg and her skeevy partner Belch die in an explosion. Belch goes to hell, but Meg's fate is not so easily decided—she ends up in limbo. St. Peter and Beelzebub give her one last chance to make good: help old man McCall complete his wish list. Meg thinks this will be easy, but Beelzebub has other plans.

Crutcher, Chris

The Sledding Hill. 2005, Greenwillow Books, ISBN: 9780060502430, 230p.

Main character Billy is dead but he's sticking around to keep an eye on his troubled best friend, Eddie. Not only has Eddie lost Billy, but his father recently passed away, too; school is not much better, as Eddie ends up with scary Mr. Tartar, who is also a brimstone-and-fire preacher. All this is too much for Eddie, who stops talking. When Mr. Tartar tries to ban a novel from school, Eddie must decide whether or not he wants to lose his voice forever.

Huntley, Amy

The Everafter. 2009, HarperCollins, ISBN: 9780061776793, 256p.

Seventeen-year-old Madison is dead, but she doesn't know how it happened. She finds herself in an undefined universe, bewildered by various objects floating around her. Only when she touches these objects—a hair clip, for example—does she realize these are items she lost when she was alive, and touching them takes her back to various scenes in her life. In this way, Madison tries to piece together what happened and what she needs to do now.

Hurley, Tonya

Ghostgirl. 2008, Little, Brown, ISBN: 9780316113571, 328p.

Charlotte User has big plans to stop being a loser and to get popular Damen to kiss her—but her plans are thwarted when she chokes to death on a gummy bear. Refusing to go peacefully into the light, Charlotte haunts her school and makes more plans—this time to possess hot-girl Scarlet's body and convince Damen to take her to the Fall Ball.

Shusterman, Neal

Everlost. Skinjacker Trilogy, 1. 2006, Simon & Schuster Books for Young Readers, ISBN: 9780689872372, 320p.

Nick and Allie die in car accidents and meet on their way toward the light. They both end up in Everlost, a sort of purgatory inhabited only by children and teens and complete with a terrifying monster named McGill. Though they are warned by Lief, a 100-year-old Afterlight, that they cannot go back to the land of the living, Allie is determined to return home. She will do anything, like make the dangerous journey from Everlost to New York, and even skinjack— inhabit a living person.

Soto, Gary
The Afterlife. 2003, Harcourt, ISBN: 9780152047740, 161p.

Seventeen-year-old Chuy is combing his hair in a nightclub bathroom when he is stabbed to death. Immediately, his spirit floats out of his body and he moves around town, observing the life he left behind. What he sees both shocks and saddens him, and he is more than happy when he meets the specter of Crystal, a girl who has killed herself. The two fall in love, but Chuy realizes he is slowly fading away, and he's not sure he's ready to go.

Zevin, Gabrielle ♔
▶ *Elsewhere.* 2005, Farrar, Straus, & Giroux, ISBN: 9780374320911, 288p.

Liz Hall is 15 years old with her whole life ahead of her—then she is hit and killed by a taxi. Thrust into a strange afterlife called Elsewhere, where people age backwards from the time of the deaths, Liz discovers that Elsewhere is kind of like earth with its friendships, family members, and longings. In spite of her new circumstances, Liz won't let go of the life she left behind.

Hanging with the King: Arthurian Fantasy

Intrigued by that misunderstood wizard Merlin? Want to know more about the magical sword Excalibur? How about Guinevere, or Morgan le Fey? You'll find traditional Arthurian characters here as well as reimagined ones. And if you've never read King Arthur stories before, hang onto your suit of armor and enjoy the ride.

Baron, T. A.
Child of the Dark Prophecy. Great Tree of Avalon, 1. 2004, Philomel Books, ISBN: 9780399237638, 432p.

A dark prophecy foretells of Avalon's doom; a child born 17 years earlier will be the bringer of destruction, and at the same time Merlin's heir will be revealed. Scree, an orphaned eagleboy, was raised with Tamwyn, but the two are now separated. Scree is guarding Merlin's staff, while Tamwyn starts off on a journey to stop the prophecy—for he is sure he is the Dark Child.

Clement-Davies, David
The Telling Pool. 2005, Abrams, ISBN: 9780810957589, 360p.

During the reign of Richard the Lionhearted, Rhodri is a young, Welsh falconer whose father has gone to fight in the Crusades. Through a fortune-teller, Rhodri learns of an evil war looming on the horizon and the part that he is to play in it. He is descended from Guinevere, of Arthurian times, and with the aid of the mystical Telling Pool, his falcon, and a legendary sword, Rhodri must try to save all that he knows and loves from impending doom.

Holland-Crossley, Kevin ♛
The Seeing-Stone. Arthur Trilogy, 1. 2000, Orion Children's Books, ISBN: 9781858813974, 324p.

Thirteen-year-old Arthur lives in an English manor in the 12th century and hopes to become a squire rather than a scholar. Another boy named Merlin gives him the gift of an obsidian stone, and Arthur begins to see images in it—events from the life of another boy with the same name. As Arthur records all that happens in his diary, he wonders how he and the Arthur in the stone are connected, and if his own destiny may lie beyond that of just a squire.

Spinner, Stephanie
Damosel: In Which the Lady of the Lake Renders a Frank and Often Startling Account of Her Wondrous Life and Times. 2008, Alfred A. Knopf, ISBN: 9780375936340, 224p.

Damosel is a Lady of the Lake, commissioned by Merlin to make the magical sword Excalibur for the future King Arthur. She is further entreated to care for Arthur with her magical abilities when he is in court. Also part of the story is Twixt, a dwarf, also serving in King Arthur's court. Together, dwarf and water spirit reveal life under political intrigue and how best to break the rules.

Vande Velde, Vivian
The Book of Mordred. 2005, Houghton Mifflin, ISBN: 9780618507542, 342p.

Camelot is falling to dark forces. When she is five years old, Kiera is kidnapped by an evil wizard who covets her power to see into the future. Her mother, Alyana, beseeches a knight of the Round Table, Sir Mordred, to help. Though she is rescued, Kiera cannot stop the visions, especially the one that reveals Sir Mordred as a traitor.

Yolen, Jane ♛
▶ *Sword of the Rightful King: A Novel of King Arthur.* 2003, Harcourt, ISBN: 9780152025274, 349p.

To win the favor of the kingdom, Merlinnus the mage decides on a task for King Arthur: remove a sword from a stone to show that he is the rightful heir. Arthur's evil half-sister, the witch Morgause, wants one of her own sons on the throne. She sends 17-year-old Gawaine and three of his brothers to Camelot. Divided loyalties and an assassination plot all muddle things—especially when someone unexpected retrieves the sword.

Something's Afoot: Magic and Mystery

If you think about it, *all* magic is mysterious by its very nature. Add crime, murder, and general mayhem, and you get mystery stories that even Sherlock Holmes would have a rough time deciphering.

Devlin, Ivy

Low Red Moon. 2010, Bloomsbury Children's Books, ISBN: 9781599905105, 208p.

Seventeen-year-old Avery witnesses her parents' gruesome murders but she can't remember anything about it. Shuttled off to live with a grandmother she's never known, Avery wanders through school confused and sorrowful, until she meets a mysterious new boy, Ben of the silver eyes. Slowly, Avery begins to piece together the events of that horrible night and wonders if she can truly trust Ben at all.

Kirby, Matthew

The Clockwork Three. 2010, Scholastic Press, ISBN: 9780545203371, 386p.

Three down-and-out kids, Giuseppe, Frederick, and Hannah, all have dreams to escape their horrible lives in a 19th-century alternative Victorian America. But each of their dreams contains mysteries that can only be solved by the others' help. Their lives soon merge together as they work to make all their dreams a reality.

Kittredge, Caitlin

The Iron Thorn. Iron Codex, 1. 2011, Delacorte, ISBN: 9780385907200, 512p.

In an alternate 1950s, Aoife Grayson fears the hereditary madness that seems to strike her family members at age 16. She vows to leave the totalitarian city of Lovecraft in search of a father she's never known and to solve the mystery of her brother's disappearance—which lands her into the magical world of Thorn.

Perez, Marlene

Dead Is the New Black. Dead Is—, 1. 2008, Harcourt, ISBN: 9780152064082, 190p.

Seventeen-year-old Daisy Giordano lives in Nightshade, California, and comes from a family of supernaturally talented individuals: her mother and sisters are psychic, though Daisy is not. When looking dead becomes the new norm, Daisy suspects something evil—and she's right—vampires have come to Nightshade. She and her sisters launch on a psychic detective adventure to stop the vampire from attacking all of the school's cheerleaders.

Peterson, Will

Triskellion. 2008, Candlewick Press, ISBN: 9780763639716, 365p.

Fourteen-year-old twins Rachel and Adam leave behind divorcing parents in Manhattan to spend the summer in the English countryside with their grandmother. The village seems unassuming, but all that changes when a television show archaeology crew digs up an old relic—a three-bladed talisman, the Triskellion. Soon the twin realize that the villagers—including their own grandmother—will go to great lengths to protect an old secret.

Pierce, Tamora

▶ *Magic Steps. Circle Opens, 1.* 2000, Scholastic Press, ISBN: 9780590396059, 264p.

Sandry is 14 and no stranger to magic. She unwillingly accepts a pupil, Pasco, and is mentoring him when a family in Summersea is murdered by invisible killers. Sandry and Pasco then undergo a dangerous mission to capture the killers and save more families from a similar fate.

Sampson, Jeff
Vesper: A Deviants Novel. 2011, Balzer & Bray, ISBN: 9780061992766, 304p.

Sixteen-year-old Emily, who has always been shy and geeky, suddenly becomes a violent party girl at night after the murder of a classmate. When daylight returns, Emily is bewildered by her wild behavior, and she becomes determined to learn what is happening to her—and if the changes are happening to any of her other classmates.

Struggling with Our Demons: Battling Evil Fiends

Lots of us have hellish jobs, but imagine if fighting demons and outsmarting Satan were part of your duties. These stories take us to places of fire, brimstone, and beyond.

Barnes, Jennifer Lynn
Every Other Day. 2011, Egmont USA, ISBN: 9781606841693, 336p.

Kali is 16 and dealing with typical high school problems—parents, mean girls, grades. Every other day, however, Kali deals with being a demon hunter. On these days, her supernatural powers kick in and she hunts the marked. Things get complicated when she sees the mark of death on popular girl's back, and soon she is thick in the middle of a scientific conspiracy.

Brennan, Sarah Rees ♈
The Demon's Lexicon. Demon's Lexicon Trilogy, 1. 2009, Margaret K. McElderry Books, ISBN: 9781416963790, 322 p.

Sixteen-year-old Nick is always on the run with his family, ever since his father was murdered. They are marked, since his mother stole a powerful charm that is sought by many an evil magician, and so they must fight demons constantly. They've become used to their lives, and all is upset by the arrival of two teenagers seeking their help.

Clare, Cassandra
▶ *City of Bones. Mortal Instruments, 1.* 2008, Margaret K. McElderry, ISBN: 9781416955078, 512p.

One night, Clary witnesses three tattooed teenagers murder another teen, but the murder victim vanishes before her eyes. She learns the teens are Shadowhunters, part of a supernatural group charged with killing demons. When Clary returns home, she finds her apartment destroyed, her mother kidnapped, and a giant, slimy creature ready to kill her. Clary is swept into the complicated and dark world of the Shadowhunters as she tries to find her mom and learns about her heritage.

Gill, David Macinnis 🏆
Soul Enchilada. 2009, Greenwillow Books, ISBN: 9780061673023, 368 p.

Eighteen-year-old Bug has just graduated high school and doesn't have much going for her in the world, except her car. Given to her by her grandfather, Bug loves her 1958 Cadillac Biarritz and is less than thrilled when a demon appears demanding to repossess it. Turns out Bug's grandpa financed the car by selling his soul to Satan. After some fast talking, Bug is given two days' grace in which she frantically searches for her missing grandpa and thinks up ways to dupe the devil.

Oliver, Jana G.
The Demon Trapper's Daughter. 2011, St. Martin's Griffin, ISBN: 9780312614782, 355p.

Seventeen-year-old Riley Blackthorne has apprenticed at her father's side, hunting the demons that run amuck in 2018 Atlanta, Georgia. When her father is killed, Riley's life is thrown into turmoil. Beck, former partner to Mr. Blackthorne, steps in to continue Riley's training, though she despises him. On top of everything is the plot against Riley—someone has told the demons her name.

Shan, Darren
Demon Thief. Demonata, 2. 2006, Little, Brown, ISBN: 9780316012379, 256p.

Kernel has the strange power of opening up windows into other dimensions. Unwittingly, he releases a demon, who kidnaps his baby brother. The family is tormented by both grief and by the released demon, until Kernel learns that he is a Disciple, meant to hunt down and destroy the powerful Demonata.

Messin' with Mother Nature: Earthly Disasters

Throwing trash out a car window or dumping oil into the ocean is just not cool. As far as we know, this is the only earth we get, so we better respect it while we still can! These novels deal with the fallout of mistreating our planet.

Bell, Hilari
Trickster's Girl. Raven Duet, 1. 2010, Houghton Mifflin, ISBN: 9780547196206, 281p.

It's the year 2098 and—no surprise—humans have pretty much destroyed the earth, causing all sorts of horrific things like cancer and dying forests to spike. Fifteen-year-old Kelsa has lost her dad and is angry with her mom, so when a young man named Raven invites her along on a magical journey to heal the earth, she agrees. Traveling from Utah to Alaska is hard enough, but then other forces intervene—forces who believe earth would be better off without humans.

Bertagna, Julie
Exodus. 2008, Walker, ISBN: 9780802797452, 352p.
　　　Much of the earth's surface is underwater due to global warming. When 15-year-old Mara's small island is submerged, she leads her community across the vast oceans to a walled city called New Mungo. New Mungo, however, has an elitist, complicated caste system, and Mara and her people are stranded. To stop their imminent deaths, Mara must find a way over the wall and enlist help.

Falkner, Brian
The Tomorrow Code. 2008, Random House, ISBN: 9780375939235, 368p.
　　　Friends Tane and Rebecca, two New Zealand teenagers, uncover a strange SOS consisting mostly of 0s and 1s. They puzzle it out and realize it's a desperate message sent by themselves from the future, warning of a horrific biological disaster. They set out on a quest to stop an impending ecological disaster that could mean the end of humanity.

James, Nick
The Pearl Wars. Skyship Academy, 1. 2011, Flux, ISBN: 9780738723419, 376p.
　　　In 2095, earth's only energy source comes from space debris called Pearls. Fifteen-year-old Jesse reluctantly attends Skyship Academy, but things change when he learns he can control the Pearls. This interests members of the Unified Party, who want to capture him. Jesse finds himself relying on the friendship of Cassius, a kid who has been trained as a spy.

Mullin, Mike
Ashfall. Ashfall Trilogy, 1. 2011, Tanglewood, ISBN: 9781933718552, 476p.
　　　Iowan teenager Alex is home alone when the Yellowstone supervolcano erupts, causing the weather to go berserk and coating everything in layers of ash. Determined to find his family, who went visiting in nearby Illinois, Alex sets out on a harrowing journey across a vastly altered landscape and crosses paths with desperate people. Only his wits and the occasional good-hearted person, such as mechanically inclined Darla, help him navigate in this grim survival tale.

Stracher, Cameron
The Water Wars. 2011, Sourcebooks Fire, ISBN: 9781402243691, 240p.
　　　In the future, water has become scarce and precious. Siblings Vera and Will's mother is actually dying for want of clean water, and when they meet Kai, whose father is a water driller, they are fascinated and hopeful by his presence.

When Kai is abducted, Vera and Will set out to find him, crossing through the once United States and into Canada, where they encounter the Bluewater, an organization that has monopolized the water desalinization process.

Weyn, Suzanne
▶ *Empty.* 2010, Scholastic Press, ISBN: 9780545172783, 183p.
    Oil supplies have run out, and America has invaded Venezuela, the last country to have oil reserves. Global warming has created a super hurricane that is devastating the east coast. A group of vastly different teens—Gwen, Tom, Niki, Carlos, Brock, and Hector—are trying to deal with everyday concerns, even as food and gas supplies dwindle. Desperate to find hope as the end of the world looms near, Gwen stumbles across a secret that just might save them all.

You Give Me Fever: Plague Stories

In our society where everybody carries hand sanitizer, it's hard for us to imagine a super-germ wiping out most of humanity, but that's exactly what happens in these stories. It's the Black Plague times a billion.

Hautman, Pete
Hole in the Sky. 2001, Simon & Schuster for Young Readers, ISBN: 9780689831188, 179p.
    The world's population has been ravaged by a super flu. To avoid the virus, Ceej, his sister, and his uncle have settled near the Grand Canyon. Meanwhile, a cult of religious zealots who have managed to remain immune to the virus use the flu to malicious ends. When Ceej's family disappears, he fears the Kinkas have taken them. This sets him off on a rescue mission with his friend, Tim, and a young Hopi girl who believes she knows the way out of the diseased world.

Hirsch, Jeff
The Eleventh Plague. 2011, Scholastic Press, ISBN: 9780545290142, 304p.
    Twenty years ago, war and a devastating plague have wiped out almost all of humanity; this is known as the Collapse. Survivors, like 15-year-old Stephen and his father, roam the country as scavengers and largely avoid other survivors. When Stephen's father is injured, they find themselves living in a gated community that mimics life before the Collapse, complete with school, holidays, and sports. Stephen is suspicious of the group's leader, and his worries are validated with Jenny, an outcast also living in this utopia.

Lu, Marie
▶ *Legend.* 2011, G. P. Putnam's Sons, ISBN: 9780399256752, 336p.
    North America has split into two warring nations, due to global warming and plagues. Teenager Day, a futuristic Robin Hood who steals from the rich to

help the poor, is a wanted criminal. June is a prodigy being trained as an elite spy and warrior for the Republic. The two come face-to-face after both experience personal tragedies, and they are shocked when they realize all is not as it seems in the black-and-white worlds.

Meyer, Marissa
Cinder. Lunar Chronicles, 1. 2012, Feiwel & Friends, ISBN: 9780312641894, 400p.

Cinder is a young mechanic and cyborg doggedly working for her ruthless stepmother in New Beijing. The aftermath of World War IV has destroyed much of the earth, along with the plague known as lutemosis. Thinking her life will never change, Cinder has a chance meeting with Prince Kai and glimpses a bit of hope for the future. But then, evil Lunar Queen Levana arrives on earth, and her sights are set on the prince.

Stephens, J. B.
The Big Empty. Big Empty, 1. 2004, Razorbill, ISBN: 1595140069, 204p.

After a plague kills off most of humanity, a dictatorship rises to power in the former United States and moves all the survivors to the coasts, away from what is known as The Big Empty. Seven teenagers, all outcasts in various ways, come together searching for a better way of life. Keely, Jonah, and Irene have heard of Novo Mundum, a free-thinking, artistic community that is against martial law, and Diego, Michael, Amber, and Maggie decide to join them.

Treggiari, Jo
Ashes, Ashes. 2011, Scholastic Press, ISBN: 9780545255639, 352p.

The weather has gone berserk, and thanks to a smallpox epidemic, most of mankind has died off. Small groups of survivors live across the country, including 16-year-old Lucy, who hides out in what's left of New York's Central Park. Lucy meets Aidan and joins his group, but they are attacked by the Sweepers, who kidnap healthy people for experimentation. Soon Lucy realizes the Sweepers are interested in her for more than one reason—her blood might hold an antidote to the epidemic.

Not Raised in a Barn: Fantastical Animals

Lions and tigers and flying horses, oh my! For the animal lover in you, these stories will amaze, delight, and leave you longing for a talking bear of your own.

George, Jessica Day ♛
▶ *Sun and Moon, Ice and Snow.* 2008, Bloomsbury, ISBN: 9781599901091, 328p.

The Lass is the ninth child of an impoverished family and has never received a name from her disappointed mother. The Lass blooms in other ways, however: under the steady love of an older brother and with the animals around her, for she can understand their speech. When a polar bear arrives and tells the family they will have riches and luxury if only the Lass will live with him for a year, the Lass finds herself on a journey across the frozen north.

Harrison, Mette Ivie
The Princess and the Hound. 2007, Eos, ISBN: 9780061131875, 410p.

Prince George can understand animals, a talent punishable by death in his kingdom, so he keeps his gift well hidden. Political events see him betrothed to an enemy king's daughter—a silent girl who won't travel without her hound. Bound to her by duty, George soon realizes he admires this strong-willed girl, and he also understands he must change his people's persecution.

McKinley, Robin
Pegasus. 2010, G. P. Putnam's Sons, ISBN: 9780399246777, 400p.

After years of destruction at the hands of more violent creatures, the pegasi agree to an alliance with humans, with the hope of saving their race. Dazzled by the mighty pegasi, the humans agree, but they can barely communicate through use of their magicians. It is only when Princess Sylvi turns 12 and is ceremonially bound to the Pegasus Ebon that everything changes. Sylvi and Ebon form an instant telepathic bond—something unheard of—which everyone finds threatening.

Pierce, Meredith Ann 🏆
Treasure at the Heart of the Tanglewood. 2001, Viking, ISBN: 9780670892471, 241p.

Young Hannah lives in Tanglewood with her animal companions and serves as the village's healer, yet the people seem to fear her. For years, Hannah has had no memory; she only knows she must serve a sinister wizard who forbids her to leave the wood. The wizard guards a mysterious treasure, and legend says only a knight can claim it. Hannah meets such a knight, one she calls Foxkith; but when his quest backfires, Hannah defies the wizard and starts on a journey to learn her true identity.

Weber, David
A Beautiful Friendship. Stephanie Harrington Books, 1. 2011, Baen Books, ISBN: 9781451637472, 376p.

Twelve-year-old Stephanie Harrington is living on the newly colonized planet Sphinx, and she's bored out of her mind. When she is attacked by a hexapuma, a strange three-legged treecat intervenes. Girl and beast bond with a special telepathic connection. When the powers that be learn of her connection to one of the planet's native species, they will stop at nothing to get at and study the treecats.

Willingham, Bill
Down the Mysterly River. 2011, Tor/Starscape, ISBN: 9780765327925, 336p.

Max "the Wolf" is a top Boy Scout who wakes up with no memory in the middle of a forest. Even weirder are the talking animals he encounters—a badger, a cat, and a bear. None of the animals know what's going on either. To make matters worse, there is a vicious group of humans known as the Blue Cutters, who, with one swipe of their swords, can change a person's (or beast's) entire personality. As Max and his new friends journey through the forest, searching for answers, they also must find ways to outsmart the Cutters.

Chapter Two

Character

Many people read in search of a compelling cast of characters. This can mean many things: characters with whom a reader can relate, or characters so different from the reader that they provide a wonderful and curious reading experience. Whatever the case, readers who are into character want to root for someone, to empathize, and maybe to vicariously learn and grow.

Speculative fiction—especially fantasy—is a near-perfect genre to find characters both relatable and not, since these are stories full of archetypes: the reluctant hero who is forced on a quest; the outcast girl who suddenly finds herself in a relationship with the town's mysterious new guy; the butt-kicking heroine who can wield a sword like nobody's business but still has a vulnerable side.

Stories that serve up characters first are featured in this chapter. Find your favorite titles and go from there, or just dive in and try something (or someone) new.

Love Bites: Vampire Relationships

Who hasn't dreamed of what it would be like to live forever—especially with the guy or girl of your dreams? So what if he drinks blood, or if she compels people with her freaky eyes? Vampire love is all about the forbidden and the impossible.

Fantaskey, Beth
> *Jessica's Guide to Dating on the Dark Side.* 2009, Harcourt, ISBN: 9780152063849, 354p.
>> Adopted 17-year-old Jessica Packwood discovers her real name is Antanasia Dragomir; at birth, she was betrothed to Lucius Vladescu, a dark and

brooding vampire prince. Fresh from Romania, Lucius arrives in America to fulfill the pact; he claims he and Jessica are from warring vampire clans, and if the betrothal doesn't happen, all hell will break loose back in the Carpathian Mountains. Logic-loving Jessica doesn't want—or believe—any of this, until she develops a strange thirst.

Klause, Annette Curtis

▶ *The Silver Kiss.* 2007, Delacorte Press, ISBN: 9780385904353, 198p.

Seventeen-year-old Zoe's mother has terminal cancer, and her father is distant when she needs him most. She has no one to turn to until she meets Simon, a gorgeous and compelling young man. Simon also harbors pain—a very *old* pain—and Zoe helps him devise a dangerous plan of revenge.

Meyer, Stephanie 🏆

Twilight. Twilight Saga. 2005, Little, Brown, ISBN: 9780316160179, 498p.

Bella Swan, 17, leaves sunny Phoenix to live with her dad in gloomy Forks, Washington. But one thing brightens her days—the incredibly handsome Edward Cullen. The two develop a magnetic attraction to one another, but Bella suspects something is not quite right with Edward—and she's determined to figure out what it is.

Robinson, A. M.

Vampire Crush. 2011, HarperTeen, ISBN: 9780061989711, 404p.

Sixteen-year-old Sophie McGee is a school journalist, and her first assignment for the new year is to interview all the new kids—but none of them want to talk. Things get even weirder when her old neighbor and crush, James, also returns to town. As Sophie investigates, she learns that all the new kids, including James, are connected—in ways that include fangs, death, and evil.

Schrieber, Ellen

Vampire Kisses: The Beginning. Vampire Kisses. 2003, HarperCollins, ISBN: 9780060093341, 197p.

Sixteen-year-old Raven, an outcast Goth, wants nothing more than to become a vampire. When a mysterious new boy moves into the town's old mansion, she hopes he is the one to fulfill her dark dreams.

Smith, L. J.

The Vampire Diaries: The Awakening. 1991, 2009, HarperTeen, ISBN: 9780061963865, 253p.

Elena Gilbert, bored, beautiful, and in her senior year, attracts the attention of two gorgeous but very different brothers—and ignites a centuries-old feud when she chooses one over the other.

Velde, Vivian Vande 🏆

Companions of the Night. 1995, Harcourt Brace, ISBN: 0152002219, 212p.

As far as 16-year-old Kerry Nowicki is concerned, there are no such things as vampires. Yet she finds herself helping Ethan, an attractive guy, escape from a group of men who claim Ethan is a vampire. Next thing Kerry knows, she is suspected to be a vampire, too, and her family is kidnapped in retaliation. Though she understands there is danger surrounding Ethan, Kerry knows she needs his help if she ever wants to see her family again.

My Poor Cold Heart: The Lives of the Undead

Vampires are people, too, right? Well, not really. But the ones in these novels struggle with a surprising amount of universal teenage concerns—like identity, sibling rivalry, social status, and protecting one's skin from the sun.

Anderson, M. T.
Thirsty. 2010, Macmillan Publishers, ISBN: 9780802720740, 248p.

Chris is just trying to deal with high school when his blood lust kicks in. He's always known about vampires living in his Massachusetts town, but they are a weak bunch whose leader is banished to another dimension. Though the cravings get harder to ignore, Chris tries. Then he gets a visit from Chet—a being from the Forces of Light—who wants to enlist Chris's help in freeing the vampire lord.

Block, Francesca Lia
Pretty Dead. 2009, HarperTeen, ISBN: 9780061547850, 195p.

Charlotte is a vampire living alone in a stunning mansion. Though she's gorgeous and surrounded by beautiful things, she is lonely. When her best human friend Emily kills herself, she is drawn to Emily's boyfriend, Jared, and begins to share her past with him. But Charlotte suspects the unimaginable— that she is turning back into a human.

Brewer, Heather
Eighth Grade Bites. The Chronicles of Vladimir Tod, 1. 2007, Dutton Children's Books, ISBN: 9780525478119, 182p.

Vlad is 13 years old and a vampire—sort of. His dad was all vampire; his mom was human, and since they both died while he was a baby, he never got to ask them exactly *what* he is. He has a craving for blood, which his guardian, nurse Aunt Nelly, brings home from the hospital for his consumption. Other than that, he's like every other kid in eighth grade. Then his English teacher disappears, and the creepy substitute seems to know a lot about Vlad.

De la Cruz, Melissa
Blue Bloods. 2006, Hyperion Books for Children, ISBN: 9780786838929, 302p.

These rich and beautiful teenagers who attend the prestigious Duchesne School also happen to be vampires—Blue Bloods—named for the bright blue veins that show in their arms at age 15 when their vampirism rises. Though Schuyler comes from a long line of distinguished Blue Bloods, she is considered an outsider by the clique. When the Silver Bloods begin murdering the teens, their way of life is threatened forever.

Harvey, Alyxandra

▶ *Hearts at Stake*. 2010, Macmillan Publishers, ISBN: 9780802720740, 248p.

Solange Drake just wants to be a regular teen, but when she turns 16, she is supposed to turn into a vampire—and a vampire queen at that! This prophecy brings on suitors near and far, and also assassination attempts by the current powerful and vengeful vampire queen.

Mancusi, Mari

Boys That Bite. Blood Coven. 2006, Berkley Books, ISBN: 9780425209424, 261p.

Sixteen-year-old Sunny and her Goth twin sister Rayne are nothing alike. Thanks to Rayne, Sunny has been bitten by a vampire and has one week to try and stop her transformation as the blood-mate to Magnus, King of the Coven.

Pauley, Kimberly

Sucks to Be Me: The All-True Confessions of Mina Hamilton, Teen Vampire (Maybe). 2009, Mirrorstone, ISBN: 9780786952564, 297p.

Mina has vampire parents, who turned into vampires shortly after her birth. Now, at age 16, Mina must take classes about vampire culture and decide whether she wants to turn into a vampire, too. Complicating matters are Mina's best friend Serena, two hot vampires-to-be boys, and Mina's long-time human crush, Nathan.

Westerfeld, Scott ♛

Peeps. 2005, Razorbill, ISBN: 159514031X, 312p.

Cal Thompson is parasite positive—a peeps carrier. This disease turns people into vampires, and Cal is on a mission to contact all the girls he infected. The vampirism isn't full-blown in Cal, but he keeps to himself, though he is lonely. He begins working for Night Watch, a peeps-hunting organization, and keeps himself at arm's length from everyone, until he meets Lace, a journalist. Then Cal uncovers a conspiracy that makes him question Night Watch.

Falling for You: Immortal Beings

Some people believe we all have guardian angels watching over us. How cool would that be? Well, these stories show what happens when we fall for those guardians, who may or may not always be on the good side.

Adornetto, Alexandra
Halo. 2010, Feiwel and Friends, ISBN: 9780312656263, 484p.

Venus Cove is threatened by Dark Forces. Three angels have been sent to the town to help residents fight evil temptations. The mission gets rocky when Bethany—the youngest angel stationed at the high school—falls for bad boy Jake, who is literally a demon.

Fitzpatrick, Becca
Hush Hush. 2010, Simon & Schuster Books for Young Readers, ISBN: 9784146989417, 391p.

Self-conscious Nora never dreamed her sophomore year would include a hot and confusing relationship with Patch, the new boy with a dark past. Still, she is drawn to him, even though everyone keeps telling her to stay away—and worse—even though she can sense his dangerous intentions.

Hand, Cynthia
Unearthly. 2011, HarperTeen, ISBN: 9780061996160, 435p.

Clara Gardner is a Quartarius, a quarter-angel who begins to come into her power at age 16. Her attempts to understand her earthly purpose lead her to Wyoming, where she finally meets Christian, the boy who she is supposed to protect. She also meets Tucker, a rodeo star who keeps distracting her attention, and Angela, another angel, who supplies Clara with disturbing facts about good and evil.

Kate, Lauren
▶ *Fallen.* 2009, Delacorte Press, ISBN: 9780385738934, 452p.

Luce has been haunted by terrifying shadows all her 17 years. When she is suspected in the death of her boyfriend, she is sent to a stark and strange reform school in Georgia, where she meets two very different but equally compelling boys, and begins to learn the origins of the shadows.

Smith, Cynthia Leitich
Eternal. Tantalize Series, 2. 2009, Candlewick Press, ISBN: 9780763635732, 307p.

Miranda's guardian angel Zachary tries to save her from becoming a vampire, but fails and falls from grace. The result is that Miranda becomes a heedless vampire princess and Zachary gives up—until an archangel offers him another chance at redeeming Miranda's soul and regaining his wings.

Terrell, Heather
Fallen Angel. 2011, HarperTeen, ISBN: 9780061965708, 310p.

Sixteen-year-old Ellie has been having odd flying dreams and can read flashes of other people's thoughts. When she meets Michael, a boy from her hazy past, she discovers they share similar powers. As Ellie digs deeper, she learns she is half-human, half-angel and must choose either the dark or light side in a biblical battle that just might determine the end of days.

Weatherly, L. A.
Angel Burn. Angel Trilogy, 1. 2011, Candlewick Press, ISBN: 9780763656522,
464p.

    Angel burn is what happens when ethereal beings come to earth and
feed off humans—humans are too dazzled by the beautiful beings to notice
their fading health until it's too late. Because their own world is disintegrat-
ing, these creatures—angels—have begun to invade earth more and more.
Willow doesn't know she is half-angel; Alex is from an angel-killing organization sent to kill her. What happens when the two meet is anything but
expected.

Dangerous Beauties: The Realm of Faerie

    Gossamer, beautiful, and usually deadly, these fairies are far from the sweet
little dancing kind in children's stories. Typically unnoticed by the human eye,
these fairies dwell in realms full of court intrigue and political deception—until
they cross over to the human side.

Balog, Cyn
Fairy Tale. 2009, Delacorte Press, ISBN: 9780385737074, 248p.

    Morgan Sparks and her boyfriend Cam have been best friends since they
were children, but just before their shared 16th birthday, Cam confesses that
he is a fairy who was switched at birth with a human child, and now the fairies
want to switch them back.

Brennan, Herbie 🏆
Faerie Wars. 2003, Bloomsbury, ISBN: 1582348103, 367p.

    Henry's parents are breaking up, and he finds solace helping old Mr. Fog-
arty. Unwittingly, he saves the life of Pyrgus Malvae, the son of a Faerie King,
who has traveled through a portal to the human world. Together, boy and faerie
return to the Purple Kingdom to defeat the despicable Faeries of the Night,
who want Pyrgus dead.

Jones, Carrie
Need. 2009, Bloomsbury, ISBN: 9781599903385, 306p.

    After her stepfather dies, Zara is sent to live with her grandmother in a
little town in Maine. A car accident introduces her to Nick, a hot guy who turns
out to be a werewolf. Just as Zara thinks life might be looking up again, she
finds out she's being followed by an evil pixie king, who wants nothing less
than a blood sacrifice.

Jones, Frewin
▶ *The Faerie Path. Faerie Path, 1*. 2007, Eos, ISBN: 9780060871024, 312p.

Right before Anita turns 16, she ends up in the hospital after an accident. After dreaming of flying, she is suddenly transported out of modern London to the world of Faerie. Here she learns about her true identity: she is Tania, the long-lost seventh daughter of King Oberon. Now Anita/Tania must learn how to deal with her real identity, love her new family while still missing her old human one, and reconcile a proposed marriage to underhanded Lord Drake.

Kagawa, Julie

The Iron King. Iron Fey; Book One. 2010, Harlequin Teen, ISBN: 9780373210084, 363p.

Meghan Chase is almost 16 when strange things begin happening. She learns that her little brother, Ethan, has been kidnapped by fey. Her best friend, Robbie, turns out to be the faerie Puck from *A Midsummer Night's Dream,* and he offers to escort her into the beautiful and bizarre faerie world on a rescue mission.

Melling, O. R.

The Hunter's Moon. Chronicles of Faerie, 1. 2005, Amulet Books, ISBN: 9780810958579, 284p.

American-born Gwen and her Irish cousin Findabhair have a love for fantasy and hope to find an otherworldly door during their trip in Ireland. Little did either girl know they would do exactly that, and Findabhair is kidnapped by the King of Faerie himself. Usually cautious Gwen realizes she must shore up her courage and assemble a band of helpers to rescue her cousin from a fate worse than the darkest fantasy ever.

Pike, Aprilynne

Wings. 2009, HarperTeen, ISBN: 9780061668036, 294p.

Homeschooled till age 15, Laurel and her parents move to Los Angeles and leave behind land that has been in the family for generations. As she navigates high school, Laurel takes note of her differences—she's vegan, attracted to the outdoors, and suddenly sprouts a plant on her back. When she returns to her old home, she meets handsome faerie Tamini, who tells her of her true nature—fey.

Stiefvater, Maggie ♛

Lament: The Faerie Queen's Deception. Books of Faerie, 1. 2008, Flux, ISBN: 9780738713700, 325p.

Sixteen-year-old Deirdre Monaghan is a talented harpist struck by stage fright before every performance. While puking before a big competition, she meets handsome flutist Luke, who calms her nerves and performs a duet with her. They win the competition, and Deirdre falls hard for Luke, but her happiness is short-lived. She starts noticing four-leaf clovers everywhere, along with vicious creatures who seem otherworldly.

It's a Wizard Thing: Masters and Mages

For anyone who thinks magic comes easy, just ask these characters. Honing your wizardry skills takes practice, patience, focus—and sometimes the artful dodging of evil forces out to kill you.

Bell, Hilari
The Wizard Test. 2005, Eos, ISBN: 9780060599423, 166p.

In the land of Tharn, wizards are despised and considered untrustworthy, so 14-year-old Dayven is sickened when he learns of his own magical abilities. However, Tharn is on the brink of war with the Cenzars, a rebellious people who live beyond the walled city. Charged with the task of spying, Dayven is apprenticed to the drunken wizard Reddick Dayven. As time passes, he finds he likes the Cenzars *and* the master wizard, and begins to question everything he's ever known.

Chima, Cinda Williams
The Warrior Heir. Heir Trilogy, 1. 2006, Hyperion Books for Children, ISBN: 9780786839162, 426p.

Sixteen is too young for a heart condition, but Jack takes medicine for one every day. When he forgets his medicine one morning, he exhibits mega-strength at soccer tryouts, and the secret about his ancestry is revealed—he is a Warrior Heir, and the medicine was designed to suppress his powers until he could receive adequate training. That training includes a magic sword, dodging evil strangers, and preparing for a death duel.

Duane, Diane
So You Want To Be a Wizard. Young Wizards, Book 1. 2001, Harcourt, ISBN: 0152012397, 385p.

Thirteen-year-old Nita seeks refuge from school bullies in the library. There she finds a book called *So You Want To Be a Wizard,* and even though she thinks it's a joke, she checks it out. The next day she meets Kit Rodriguez, and together they begin working on spells. Soon they are doing things like talking to trees and calling forth creatures from other dimensions (Fred, a white hole). When they slide into an alternate Manhattan, their new skills are put to the test, as they must defeat the evil Lone Power.

Duey, Kathleen
Skin Hunger. Resurrection of Magic; Book 1. 2007, Atheneum Books for Young Readers, ISBN: 9780689840944, 357p.

Two stories happen in this book—the first one belongs to Sadima, who grows up on a farm and has the ability to hear the thoughts of animals. When she takes to the city, she meets Franklin and Somiss, both who are working to save magic. The next story happens generations later and features Hahp, an unfortunate boy who is sent to a magician's academy run by none other than

Somiss and Franklin. There are no lovely feasts at this school—if the boys cannot conjure their own meals, they starve to death. As conditions worsen, Hahp begins to believe the rumor that only one boy will survive to become a wizard.

LeGuin, Ursula K.

A Wizard of Earthsea. Earthsea Quartet; Book 1. 1991, Atheneum, ISBN: 0689317204, 197p.

Ged, otherwise known as Sparrowhawk, is a reckless boy living north of Earthsea. By accident, he discovers he has magical talents and uses them to rid his village of raiders. Ogion, a wise old mage, takes Ged on to train him, but old habits die hard, and in his impatience, Ged summons up a strange shadow being and unleashes its evil on the world. Now he must figure out a way to destroy the shadow once and for all.

Rowling, J. K. 🏆

▶ *Harry Potter and the Sorcerer's Stone.* 1997, Arthur A. Levine Books, ISBN: 9780590353403, 309p.

Eleven-year-old Harry Potter lives in utter neglect with his peevish aunt, uncle, and fat cousin Dudley. Harry knows he has always been different, but things get worse when he unwittingly releases a snake from the zoo. He is rescued by a giant of a man named Hagrid, who informs Harry that he is a wizard and is going to attend the Hogwarts School of Witchcraft and Wizardry. The wonder and excitement of Harry's new-found life is tempered by learning that an evil wizard, Lord Voldemort, was responsible for the death of his parents.

Sage, Angie

Magyk. Septimus Heap Book 1. 2005, Katherine Tegen Books, ISBN: 9780060577315, 564p.

Septimus Heap, the seventh son of a seventh son, is destined to do great things—except he is born and dies in the very first chapter! Enter Jenna, the 10-year-old orphan adopted by the Heap family. When an assassination attempt is made on Jenna's life, she learns her true identity—the daughter of the murdered queen. She is whisked away to safety, accompanied by family, friends, and a young army guard known as "Boy 412." Magyk abounds as Jenna and Boy 412 fight dangerous obstacles and enemies.

Stroud, Jonathan 🏆

Amulet of Samarkand. Bartimaeus Trilogy, 1. 2003, Hyperion Books for Children, ISBN: 9780786818594, 464p.

In an alternative London, Parliament is ruled by wizards. When he is five years old, Nathaniel's parents sell him to the government, where he is apprenticed to a cold wizard named Mr. Underwood. Fueled by hurt and anger, Nathaniel studies magic beyond his assignments and becomes quite powerful, so much that he is able to summon a 5,000-year-old djinn named Bartimaeus to steal the infamous Amulet of Samarkand from a powerful magician.

Did I Do That? Paranormal Powers

Everyone has talents, but the characters in these stories have powers—real powers—that are usually cool, sometimes wonderful, and almost always desired by others with nefarious intentions.

Anderson, M. T.
The Secret Hour. Midnighters, 1. 2004, Eos, ISBN: 9781435248267, 297p.

If 15-year-old Jessica Day was unhappy about moving to Bixby, Oklahoma, she is even more bummed out when she discovers her magical powers. Jessica is a Midnighter, a person whose birth at exactly midnight allows her to move about in a mysterious 25th hour. As Jessica tries to become accustomed to this ability, she meets others like her—Dess, Rex, and Melissa—and learns that her arrival in Bixby has stirred up a strange breed of predators from this lost hour.

Gould, Stephen
Jumper. 2002, Starscape, ISBN: 0765342286, 345p.

Trying to escape a beating from his father, 17-year-old Davy jumps—literally—out of his home and into the town library. He can teleport! Afraid his father will track him down, Davy hides out in New York, living on the streets and using his power to survive. Eventually he teleports inside a bank and steals the money, becoming a millionaire. All of this begins to attract the attention of the U.S. government, who want Davy to work for them. Kidnappings, terrorists, questions of ethics, and a dash of romance for Davy, all follow.

Grant, Michael
Gone. 2008, HarperTeen, ISBN: 9780061448768, 447p.

Sam Temple is sitting in class one day when the teacher just disappears. He soon discovers that everyone over the age of 14 in his small California town are gone—no explanation, just gone. Everything falls into chaos; animals are mutating, and some of the kids have developed strange powers. Then the kids from Coates Academy come into town, and Caine, a little bully with kinetic powers, takes over with brute force.

Jones, Patrick
The Tear Collector. 2009, Walker and Company, ISBN: 9780802787101, 263p.

Cass Gray is 17 and works tirelessly as a volunteer grief counselor. She always lends a shoulder to cry on—and this is imperative for her survival, because Cass is a grief vampire. She and her family depend on human tears to live, and so she collects as many as she can and brings them home. Her family expects her to wed her cousin and give birth to an heir, but lately, Cass has been wondering what it's like to be human. When she falls in love with a boy named Scott, she finds herself in the impossible situation of having to choose between her best interests and her family.

McMann, Lisa

Wake. 2008, Simon Pulse, ISBN: 9781416953579, 210p.

High school senior Janie has a secret: ever since she was eight years old, she has been pulled unwillingly into other people's dreams. Whenever people fall asleep near her, Janie enters their dreams or nightmares and suffers terrible side effects. When she enters loner Cabel's dreams, she learns of his abusive childhood and something even more disturbing. In spite of this, Janie and Cabel begin a tentative romance, and she slowly understands how she can put her powers to good use.

Ward, Rachel ♔

▶ *Num8ers.* 2010, Chicken House/Scholastic, ISBN: 9780545142991, 325p.

Fifteen-year-old Jem Marsh knew when her drug-addicted mother would die—she could see the exact date in her mother's eyes. In fact, Jem can see everybody's death date stamped in their eyes, so she avoids looking at people and keeps herself distanced from relationships. When she meets gangly, infectious Spider, Jem decides to throw caution to the wind and go with him to London for a little fun. All that changes when she sees the death date of all the tourists waiting in line for the London Eye Ferris wheel.

Meet the Orphans

Just the word orphanage is creepy—it conjures up images of torture, dirt, and gruel for dinner, and we instantly feel bad for any kid who is parentless. But sometimes, orphanages and their inmates can be special.

Almond, David ♔

Heaven Eyes. 2001, Delacorte Press, ISBN: 9780385327701, 233p.

Erin and her friends January and Mouse escape from an orphanage for damaged children and sail down the river on a homemade raft. They land on the Black Middens, a mud bank inhabited by a demented old man ("Grandpa") and the child he rescued from the mud long ago. The child is called Heaven Eyes, and she speaks a strange, almost musical dialect; she also has webbed fingers. Erin and the others fall into an idyllic life on the mud bank, until Grandpa dies.

Cornish, D. M. ♔

Foundling. Monster Blood Tattoo, 1. 2006, G. P. Putnam's Sons, ISBN: 9780399246388, 434p.

Poor Rossamund—not only does he have a girl's name but he's also an orphan living in a home for foundlings. When he is given a job as a lamplighter, he must roam the monster-strewn roads of Half-Continent every night. Humans and monsters are constantly battling in this violent place; when a monster is destroyed, the human killer receives a tattoo made from that creature's blood. Rossamund is drawn to the idea of fighting monsters, and he gets his chance when he meets up with Europe, a slayer from an elite society.

Jean, Mark
Puddlejumpers. 2008, Hyperion Books for Children, ISBN: 9781423107590, 328 p.

When he was just an infant, Ernie was kidnapped by Puddlejumpers—11-inch-tall elven creatures who live beneath puddles. They believe he is their "Rainmaker" and give him a comfortable life until their mortal enemies, the Troggs, chase him out. Now Ernie is stuck in a Chicago orphanage, dealing with a nasty supervisor and a whole lot of memories. When drought plagues the Midwest, Ernie and his new friend Joey decide to return to the Puddlejumpers and deal with the Troggs once and for all.

Lackey, Mercedes
Legacies. Shadow Grail, 1. 2010, Tor, ISBN: 9780765327079, 320p.

Sixteen-year-old Spirit loses her whole family in a car wreck. After weeks of rehabilitation, she is sent to Oakhurst Academy, a boarding school and orphanage for students with magical powers. Spirit is a legacy, meaning her folks had magic, but her powers will not manifest. She is struggling to adjust when students start disappearing, and she and her friends begin to investigate.

Riggs, Ransom
▶ *Miss Peregrine's Home for Peculiar Children.* 2011, Quirk Books, ISBN: 9781594744761, 352p.

Jacob's grandfather is a World War II veteran with a penchant for telling monster stories and showing him weird photos. Grandpa also spent some of his childhood in an orphanage in an island off the coast of Wales, where his companions supposedly had supernatural powers. Jacob chalks up Grandpa's stories as deluded ramblings—until Grandpa is murdered, and Jacob sees a monster with his own eyes. The event sends Jacob into madness, fear, and the search for truth. He travels to the old orphanage, falls into a time loop, and meets Miss Peregrine's very peculiar children.

Ruiz Zafon, Carlos
The Midnight Palace. 2011, Little, Brown, ISBN: 9780316044738, 304p.

In 1916 Calcutta, fraternal twins Sheere and Ben are orphaned when a mysterious and malevolent man murders their parents. Ben is placed in an orphanage, Sheere is spirited away by their grandmother, and the twins don't see each other again until they are 16. Sheere and their grandmother come for Ben with dark news: Jawahal, the man who killed their parents, is after them—and he is not human.

Just Like Me: Robots and Clones

With everything that needs to be done, I sometimes (okay, always) wish I had a clone, or maybe a self-sufficient robot to take care of it all. I bet some of these characters felt the same way—until they got their wish.

Brooks, Kevin
Being. 2008, Scholastic, Inc., ISBN: 9780439903424, 323p.

After a routine checkup reveals that his innards are made of metal and plastic, 16-year-old Robert panics and runs. Somehow he is accused of murder, and a covert government faction is on his tail. Not understanding who—or what—he is, Robert meets Eddi, a girl who is an expert in making fake IDs. Together they flee, hoping to escape with their lives and to find answers to Robert's questions.

Cusik, John M.
Girl Parts. 2010, Candlewick Press, ISBN: 9780763649302, 218p.

Wealthy David can't seem to feel, so his parents purchase Rose, a robot girl designed to help him regain emotions. Rose is beautiful and made to please, and she almost does the trick until David discovers she has no girl parts and discards her. Then sensitive, poor Charlie finds Rose, and boy and bot fall in love. As Rose's personality grows, she dreams of becoming a real girl—and will take steps to make that dream a reality.

Farmer, Nancy ♛
The House of the Scorpion. 2002, Atheneum Books for Young Readers, ISBN: 0689852223, 380p.

In the future, a new country springs up between the United States and Mexico, called Opium, also their major export, and tended by human drones controlled by microchips in their brains. Enter Matt, a 14-year-old clone who is a replica of El Patrón, the country's supreme ruler. Matt discovers that El Patrón has had other clones whose organs were harvested to keep the drug lord alive for 142 years. Though his life may be expendable, Matt begins to form an identity and decides to fight for it.

Haddix, Margaret Peterson
Double Identity. 2005, Simon & Schuster Books for Young Readers, ISBN: 0689873743, 218p.

A few days before Bethany turns 13, her parents suddenly deposit her at Myrlie's house, an aunt she has never known. Aunt Myrlie is startled when she sees Bethany, because Bethany is the spitting image of someone named Elizabeth. As the mysteries unfold, Bethany discovers that she is a clone of her older sister, who was killed in a car crash 20 years ago.

Lasky, Kathryn
Star Split. 1999, Hyperion Books for Children, ISBN: 0786804599, 203p.

It's the year 3038. When you are a Genhant, (genetically enhanced human) like 13-year-old Darci Murlowe, you've been implanted with a 48th chromosome, and your future is carefully planned. Superior as she may be, Darci is still fascinated by Originals, those who could not afford extra genetic material. When Darci comes face-to-face with a clone of herself, she is shocked—her parents have committed a capital crime. She also begins to wonder how alike she and her clone really are, or if all sentient life develops in its own way.

Levitin, Sonia
The Goodness Gene. 2005, Dutton Children's Books, ISBN: 05254793971, 259p.
    Twin brothers 16-year-old Will and Berk are the sons of the Compassionate Director of the Dominion of the Americas—a world where babies are genetically engineered, and all pleasure is controlled. Since they will take over their father's position someday, Will and his brother travel the Dominion to witness life in various regions. When Will meets Leora, she shows him around her colony and unveils some unsettling experiences—including a shocking discovery about himself.

McKissack, Pat
The Clone Codes. 2010, Scholastic Press, ISBN: 9780439929837, 173p.
    In the year 2170, 13-year-old Leanna attends the All-Virtual School, which allows her to study historical events by virtually being there. Then her mother is arrested for her involvement in The Liberty Bell, a secret organization pledged to free clones from slavery and abuse. Leanna is determined to save her mother, and when she learns that she, too, is a clone, her mission becomes even more vital.

Pearson, Mary 🏆
▶   *The Adoration of Jenna Fox.* 2008, Henry Holt, ISBN: 9780805076684, 272p.
    Seventeen-year-old Jenna wakes from a long coma, her memory nearly wiped out. Her parents reveal that she has been in a horrible accident; the family proceeds to move to California, and though Jenna watches family videos to try and rekindle her memory, she is instructed not to talk about the accident. Soon, pieces of her past start to return, and Jenna—whose father is a bioengineer—uncovers a terrible secret.

You're Such a Witch!

Admit it. You want to compel people to do your bidding. You want to feel magic thrumming at your very fingertips. These characters know exactly what that feels like—and sometimes it's not so great.

Bell, Hilari 🏆
The Goblin Wood. 2003, HarperCollins, ISBN: 0060513721, 294p.
    Makenna is a 12-year-old hedgewitch whose mother has been executed for practicing forbidden magic. The Heirarch has decided to control all power except for their own, and they deal out harsh punishment for those who disobey. Bent on revenge, Makenna runs into the woods, where she meets a tribe

of goblins who are being wiped out by the Heirarch. Together, they plan to fight, but then Tobin, a young knight, is sent to capture her.

Cabot, Meg
Jinx. 2007, HarperTeen, ISBN: 9780060837648, 262p.

Jean "Jinx" Honeychurch has earned her nickname, since bad luck follows her everywhere. To get away from a stalking boyfriend, Jinx leaves small-town Iowa to stay with her aunt in swanky Manhattan. There she is reminded by her extremely mature and not-so-nice cousin Tory that they are descended from a witch, and Tory is dabbling in black magic.

Hearn, Julie ♛
The Minister's Daughter. 2005, Atheneum Books for Young Readers, ISBN: 9780689876905, 263p.

In 1645 England, pagan beliefs and Puritan ways don't mix well. When the minister's daughter, Grace, gets herself in trouble with a village boy, she turns to the healer's granddaughter, Nell, for help. When Nell refuses to assist, Grace, her younger sister, and their friends take revenge by claiming Nell and her grandmother are witches.

MacCullough, Carolyn
Once a Witch. 2009, Clarion Books, ISBN: 9780547223995, 292p.

Seventeen-year-old Tamsin is the only person in her magical family born without a Talent. Then a Scottish stranger named Alistair shows up, assuming that Tamsin is her Talented older sister Rowena, and enlists her help in locating a family heirloom. Caught up in the excitement, Tamsin doesn't correct Alistair, and she brings her Talented friend Gabriel along for a journey back in time. Little does she realize that her actions can very well lead to the destruction of her entire family.

Pratchett, Terry ♛
▶ *The Wee Free Men. The Discworld Series.* 2003, HarperCollins, ISBN: 0060012374, 263p.

Tiffany Aching, a young witch-in-training, is minding her own business on her father's sheep farm when a monster kidnaps her little brother Wentworth. On her way to rescue him, Tiffany runs into the Wee Free Men, a band of fierce, six-inch-tall pictsies, who decide to help. Things get complicated when Tiffany has to face the evil fairy queen—on her own.

Rees, Celia ♛
Witch Child. 2001, Candlewick Press, ISBN: 0763614211, 261p.

Mary is only 14 when her grandmother is hanged for being a witch in 17th-century England. Fearful that her own powers will be discovered, she sails to Colonial America and tries for a new life in a Puritan Massachusetts village. Soon, though, her friendship with the Native Americans and her familiarity with the land arouse suspicion, especially in the Puritan girls—who begin acting strangely.

Tiernan, Cate
A Chalice of Wind. Balefire No. 1. 2005, Razorbill, ISBN: 159514045X, 2501p.
Separated at birth, twins Thais and Clio don't meet until they are 17. Up to that point, Thais has been living with her father in Connecticut, while Clio and her grandmother, a practicing witch, lived in New Orleans. After her father's death, Thais moves to New Orleans; the girls meet; and magic and mystery begin to follow them everywhere.

You Talkin' To Me? Tough Chicks

If you want female protagonists who are shrinking violets, content to sit quietly in the corner while their male counterparts take all the glory, look elsewhere. Fierce, independent *girls* populate these pages. Don't try to save their honor, or they might karate chop you in the throat.

Cashore, Kristin 🏆
Graceling. 2008, Harcourt, ISBN: 9780152063962, 471p.
In the Seven Kingdoms, children are born with special talents called Graces. Katsa has been born with the Killing Grace. Her corrupt uncle, King Randa, makes use of Katsa's talent by turning her into his henchwoman, punishing citizens for misdeeds. To stave off her guilt, Katsa runs an underground organization that fights against corrupt power. When she meets Po, a foreign prince with his own Grace, Katsa wonders if she might be strong enough to stand up to her uncle.

Collins, Suzanne 🏆
The Hunger Games. Hunger Games Trilogy, 1. 2008, Scholastic Press, ISBN: 9780439023481, 374p.
Sixteen-year-old Katniss lives in Panem, a post-apocalyptic country with a Capitol and 12 districts. All the districts are poor, a condition regulated by the rulers in the capital. Every year, each district must select by lottery two teenagers, a male and a female, to compete in the televised Hunger Games. Katniss is skilled in tracking and hunting, so when her younger sister is chosen for the Games, she takes her sister's place. What ensues is not only her fight for survival, but her ability to hold onto her humanity.

De Lint, Charles 🏆
The Blue Girl. Newford Series. 2004, Viking, ISBN: 0670059242, 368p.
Imogene is 15 and at a new high school, where her Goth look immediately labels her an outcast. She takes up with another outcast, shy Maxine, and

together they navigate through Redding High until Imogene's strong personality begins attracting more attention—of the vicious, paranormal variety.

Hale, Shannon ♛
▶ *Princess Academy.* 2005, Bloomsbury Children's Books, ISBN: 1582349932, 314p.

Miri is 14, small for her age, so her father won't let her help in the quarry, where he and the other mountain villagers mine for the prized linder stone. When the prince sends word that all girls of marrying age should attend a Princess Academy in the event that he marries one of them, Miri thinks she will finally have a chance to contribute to the family. What she doesn't count on is the long separation from her village, the cruel treatment of the prince's tutors, and her unrealized ability to communicate with the linder stone.

McKinley, Robin
Spindle's End. 2000, G. P. Putnam's Sons, ISBN: 0399234667, 422p.

Briar Rose is born a princess but cursed by Pernicia, an evil fairy. Good fairy Katriona snatches Rosie away to safety and gives her the gift of speaking to animals. As Rosie grows into a headstrong and capable girl, she has no idea of her true identity. When Pernicia learns that Rosie is alive, a battle must be fought, and Rosie meets her destiny with an assortment of animals at her side.

Nix, Garth ♛
Sabriel. Abhorsen Trilogy, 1. 1996, HarperCollins, ISBN: 0060273232, 292p.

Sabriel is the daughter of necromancer Abhorsen, and due to the dangerous nature of her father's work, she has been sent away to boarding school. When Sabriel learns that Abhorsen is missing, she must cross into the Old Kingdom, where magic is still freely used, to find him.

Courage, Lads! Boys Coming of Age

Some of us naturally take to the destiny that is laid before us, while others need a little coaxing. These titles feature boys who may not like where they are or where they are headed, but they end up embracing their identities.

Bell, Hilari
The Prophecy. 2006, Eos, ISBN: 9780060599430, 208p.

Prince Perryndon is 14 and would much rather read his books than become the warrior king that his father desires. When he finds an old scroll that describes how to kill the dragon that is wreaking havoc on the land, he decides to take hold of his destiny and slay the dragon himself, but nothing turns out the way that he thinks it should.

Flanagan, John
Ranger's Apprentice: The Ruins of Gorlan. 2005, Philomel Books, ISBN: 9781435233133, 249p.

Will is 15 and fervently hopes to become a knight, but he winds up as a Ranger's apprentice instead. Rangers are a secret group who use stealth, powers of observation, and courage to protect the kingdom, and Will realizes he is quite suited for this task. As he trains, he earns the respect of his master, and learns that his new skills will be put to the test as evil Lord Morgarath wages war on the castle.

Gruber, Michael 🏆
The Witch's Boy. 2005, Harper Tempest, ISBN: 9780060761646, 377p.

Lump is so hideously ugly that he was abandoned as an infant. A witch discovers him and decides to keep him, enlisting a bear as a nanny, and a vile djinn as a tutor. Lump grows up angry and resentful and doesn't even acknowledge when the witch sacrifices her powers to pay for his misdeeds. As he goes through various trials and tribulations, Lump finally learns what it means to be loving—and loved.

Mahy, Margaret
The Magician of Hoad. 2009, Margaret K. McElderry Books, ISBN: 9781416978077, 411p.

Heriot is 12 when his magical powers come to light, and he is forced from his farm to serve in Hoad as the king's royal magician. Once there, he is charged with reading the minds of all who visit the court. Lonely and plagued by terrible memories, Heriot befriends Cayley, a rat-of-the-city, and tries to come to terms with his inner pain.

Nix, Garth
Mister Monday. The Keys to the Kingdom, 1. 2003, Scholastic, ISBN: 9780439551236, 361p.

At the beginning of his seventh-grade school year, Arthur Penhaligon dreams that a mysterious figure hands him a key shaped like the hand of a clock. When he wakes up, he finds that the key is actually in his hand. Strange, dangerous things begin to happen all around him, and when terrifying dog-faced creatures called Fletchers attack, Arthur learns they were sent by Mister Monday, who will do anything to get his key back.

Rowling, J. K. 🏆
Harry Potter and the Goblet of Fire. Harry Potter, 4. 2000, A. A. Levine Books, ISBN: 9780439139595, 734p.

Now in his fourth year at Hogwarts School of Witchcraft and Wizardry, Harry somehow finds himself entered in the dangerous Triwizard Tournament. Lord Voldemart and his cronies use the tournament as a way to get at Harry, testing his magical talents and—after a heart-wrenching tragedy—his resolve as the only one able to kill the evil Dark Lord.

Skye, Obert
Leven Thumps and the Gateway to Foo. Leven Thumps, 1. 2005, Shadow Mountain, ISBN: 9781590383698, 342p.

    The realm of Foo is where all dreams live, and evil Sabine has been ransacking it, looking for the gateway to earth. Enter Leven Thumps, a 13-year-old who is a descendant of the gate's creator and the only one who can control it—thus keeping Sabine out. Lev and his friends find themselves on a long, twisty adventure where Lev's self-doubts are challenged in the face of danger.

Full Moon Risin': Werewolves

    Really, isn't life hard enough without changing into a lycanthrope every full moon? These characters have to deal not only with their everyday problems, but also with their wilder sides.

Barnes, Jennifer Lynn
Raised by Wolves. 2010, Egmont USA, ISBN: 9781606840597, 418p.

    When Bryn was four, she saw her parents murdered by a rogue werewolf. Raised by Callum, the alpha male of the pack, Bryn is 15 when she discovers a young man locked in Callum's basement. The young man is Chase—turned by the same rogue wolf that killed Bryn's parents. Determined to uncover as much as she can, Bryn turns her world upside down when secrets begin unfolding.

Cole, Stephen
Wounded: The Wereling. 2003, Razorbill, ISBN: 1595140417, 264p.

    While on vacation, 16-year-old Tom is attacked by a bear. Wounded, he wakes up in the middle of a remote forest, being cared for by Marcie Folan. When strange things begin to happen, such as his cravings for raw meat, Tom learns that the Folans are werewolves and have been trying to turn him into a mate for their daughter, Kate. Tom and Kate escape to New Orleans, where a witch doctor just might be able to turn him back to human.

Cremer, Andrea
Nightshade. 2010, Philomel Books, ISBN: 9780399254826, 454p.

    Werewolf Calla is betrothed to Ren, the alpha male of another werewolf pack, and they are to wed on their 18th birthday. They are all controlled by the Keepers, and Calla has never questioned their authority until she breaks the rules by saving a human boy's life. The boy, Shay, also attends Calla's school and cannot keep away from her. Soon, Calla is in love with him and must decide whether to go against the Keepers' decree or forge her own destiny.

Despain, Bree
The Dark Divine. 2010, Egmont USA, ISBN: 9781606840573, 372p.

Grace Divine is the 17-year-old daughter of a pastor, and she knows her faith is nowhere near as strong as her brother's, Jude. When a family friend, Daniel, comes back to town after an unexplained absence, Grace feels an attraction for him and learns his secret: he is a werewolf. Jude disapproves of the relationship, hinting to Grace that an ancient evil is about to be unleashed.

Klause, Annette Curtis ♛
▶ *Blood and Chocolate.* 1997, Delacorte Press, ISBN: 0385323050, 264p.

Seventeen-year-old Vivian knows what happens when werewolves and humans mix—destruction—her own father was killed by a mob. In spite of this, she develops a crush on Aiden, a meat boy, and believes that he will love her even after she reveals her true form to him. Meanwhile, Gabriel is preparing to be alpha of the pack and is determined to have Vivian as his mate.

Smith, Cynthia Leitich
Tantalize. 2007, Candlewick Press, ISBN: 9780763640590, 310p.

Quincie is 17, living with her uncle and trying to revitalize his restaurant with a vampire theme. She crushes on her best friend, Kieran, who is a hybrid werewolf-in-training, and therefore violently unpredictable at times. When the chef is murdered in a very werewolf-like way, Kieran is the prime suspect.

Stiefvater, Maggie ♛
Shiver. Wolves of Mercy Falls, 1. 2009, Scholastic, ISBN: 9780545123266, 392p.

When Grace was nine years old, a yellow-eyed wolf saved her from its wolf pack. Ever since, she has watched this wolf come and go in the woods behind her house. After a local teen is killed by wolves, Grace, now 17, worries that her beloved wolf will be hunted. When a wounded young man ends up on her back porch, Grace can't help noticing his yellow eyes. What ensues is an intense romance and a race against time.

Brains Need Not Apply: Zombies!

Everybody feels like a zombie now and then, but these characters are either running from zombies, trying to outsmart zombies, or find themselves in love with a zombie. Good luck with that, I say.

Ashby, Amanda
Zombie Queen of Newbury High. 2009, Speak, ISBN: 9780142412565, 199p.

Mia has finally been invited to the prom—by the hot football captain! When the cheerleading queen tries to steal her date, she buys a love potion from a local herbalist. Unfortunately, the spell turns Mia's entire school into zombies who have a taste for her flesh. As she tries to figure out what to do, new boy Chase appears with a few tricks up his sleeve.

James, Brian
Zombie Blondes. 2008, Feiwel and Friends, ISBN: 9780312372989, 232p.

Starting over is always painful, but 15-year-old Hannah is used to it, since she and her dad move around a lot. Her new town of Maplecrest, Vermont, poses a different kind of challenge—the cheerleading squad is comprised of zombies. But is that enough to make Hannah resist joining the pretty, popular crowd?

Jay, Stacey
You Are So Undead to Me. 2009, Razorbill, ISBN: 9781595142252, 265p.

Even though Megan is a Settler—someone who communicates with the undead—she still wants to go to the homecoming dance and join the pom squad.

When someone begins using black magic to create zombies, Megan and her friend Ethan team up to save not only lives—but the homecoming!

Maguire, Ellen
Jonas. Beautiful Dead, Book 1. 2009, Sourcebooks Fire, ISBN: 9781402239441, 271p.

Violence has suddenly plagued Ellerton High, leaving four teenagers dead. The fourth to die under strange circumstances is Jonas, Darina's boyfriend. Darina is not only heartbroken, but she can see apparitions of the recently dead teens. Soon she is on the course of righting the wrong linked to Jonas's death, so he can finally rest in peace.

Peck, Richard
Three-Quarters Dead. 2010, Dial, ISBN: 0803734549, 208p.

Sophomore Kerry is lonely and ignored until uber-popular Tanya, Makenzie, and Natalie ask her to hang out. Desperate to please them, Kerry goes along with the mean girls' every whim. Even after the three girls die in a car accident, their undead bidding compels Kerry to meet them for a pre-prom party.

Ryan, Carrie 🏆
The Forest of Hands and Teeth. Forest of Hands and Teeth, 1. 2009, Delacorte Press, ISBN: 9780385736824, 310p.

Mary lives in a fenced village in the middle of the forest. Her village is governed by the Sisterhood; beyond the fence are the Unconsecrated—undead hordes who consume flesh. When Unconsecrated batter through the fence, only Mary and five others survive, and they plunge into the forest, looking for answers and hope.

Waters, Daniel
▶ *Generation Dead.* 2008, Hyperion, ISBN: 142310921X, 392p.

Phoebe, a junior at Oakvale High, isn't too happy when dead teenagers—called "living impaired"—start returning to school. This is happening all over America, so Phoebe takes Undead Studies, the better to understand her zombie classmates, and develops a crush on Tommy, a fellow undead. Phoebe's childhood friend, Adam, is also supportive of the zombies, but he is also in love with her. Will he change his mind when the resident bully begins killing off the undead?

Looks Aren't Everything: Shape-Shifters

History is filled with stories of shape-shifters, skinwalkers, and people who can change form at will. Check out how these characters handle wings, or scales, or running on several pairs of legs.

Atwater-Rhodes, Ameila
▶ *Hawksong. Kiesha'ra, 1.* 2003, Delacorte Press, ISBN: 9780385730716, 243p.
The avians (bird shape-shifters) and the serpiente (snake shape-shifters) have been at war for so long that no one even recalls when or how it began. Princess of the avian, Danica, and prince of the serpiente, Zane, decide to marry to bring both sides to peace. But their well-meaning plan might not make it past the hate and discrimination that have plagued their people for years.

Bennett, Holly
Shapeshifter. 2010, Orca Book Publishers, ISBN: 9781554691586, 244p.
Sive has inherited magical gifts from both her parents—the power to enchant with her beautiful voice, and the power to shape-shift. It is this last power that attracts the dark lord Far Doirche, and to escape him, Sive takes refuge in the mortal world, where she lives as a deer.

Cypress, Leah
Mistwood. 2010, Greenwillow Books, ISBN: 9780061956997, 304p.
Isabel is an ancient shape-shifter charged with keeping the king of Samorna safe, but when the royal family is murdered, Isabel is found in Mistwood, wandering and with no memory. Years later, a new prince named Rokan recalls Isabel to her duty, and she struggles with her feelings for him as well as her hazy memories.

De Lint, Charles
Dingo. 2008, Firebird, ISBN: 9780142408162, 213p.
Seventeen-year-old Miguel can't help but feel attracted to the beautiful Australian girl who shows up outside his dad's comic book store with her dog. He finds out that her name is Lainey, and that she and her sister Em can shape-shift into dingoes. Things get complicated when Miguel's arch nemesis, Johnny, falls for Em. Suddenly all four are plunged into the politics and intrigue of a strange Aboriginal world.

Harrison, Mette Ivie
The Princess and the Snowbird. 2010, HarperTeen, ISBN: 9780061553172, 232p.

Jens is human with no magical talent, and Liva is the daughter of a hound and a bear, able to shape-shift to animal form. The two fall in love in spite of their apparent differences, and together the two take up against the Hunter, a vicious human intent on wiping out all of animal magic.

Jordan, Sophie
Firelight. Firelight Novels, 1. 2010, HarperTeen, ISBN: 9780061935084, 304p.

Sixteen-year-old Jacinda is a fire-breathing draki—a dragon with the ability to appear human. When her reckless flying gets her exiled to Nevada, she despairs in the desert until she meets Will. Will is a draki hunter, but Jacinda is strangely attracted to him, and this attraction is what makes her fire and dragon powers come alive.

Landon, Dena
Shapeshifter's Quest. 2005, Dutton Children's Books, ISBN: 9780525473107, 182p.

Syanthe is 18, a shape-shifter who is confined to the forest with the rest of her kind. Because the shape-shifters once rebelled, the king has them all tattooed, a mark on their faces that will poison them if they leave the forest. When her people and the forest around them fall ill, it is up to Syanthe to journey to the capital in search of a magical, healing herb—and since she escaped the tattoo mark, only she can undertake the task.

Under the Sea: Merfolk

Merfolk are fascinating creatures. Some are bubbly and fun, others are deadly. The ones in this list harbor all sorts of personalities, so take your pick. And maybe, if they start singing, you should cover your ears.

Childs, Tera Lynn
Forgive my Fins. 2010, Katherine Tegen Books, ISBN: 9780061914652, 293p.

Lily is 17, half-human and half-mermaid, and heir to the throne of the underwater kingdom Thalassinian. She is scoping out the boys in high school in order to choose a worthy mate, who will rule by her side, and all is going well—she has her eye on champion swimmer Brody. Enter obnoxious Quince, who steals much more from Lily than a kiss—her heart—and consequences abound.

Dalkey, Kara
The Ascension. Water, 1. 2002, Avon Books/HarperCollins, ISBN: 9780064408080, 235p.

Nia has just turned 16 and hopes to become an Avatar—a mermaid who protects the underwater city of Atlantis. When her wishy-washy cousin is chosen as her clan's Avatar, Nia starts to see her perfect city in a different light, especially when she discovers a cruel underwater prison and learns of her family's twisted Atlantean politics.

Dunmore, Helen
▶ *Ingo. Ingo, 1.* 2006, HarperCollins, ISBN: 9780060818524, 336p.

Sapphy and her brother Conor live on the coast of Cornwall, where their father tells them about an underwater world called Ingo. Then Dad disappears, and the siblings know it has something to do with merfolk. Their suspicions are confirmed as Sapphy and her brother go underwater and discover Ingo. As Sapphy continues to search for her dad, her mother has some odd reservations about it all, testing family bonds and Sapphy's loyalties.

Friedman, Aimee
Sea Change. 2009, Point, ISBN: 9780439922289, 320p.

Sixteen-year-old Miranda is a lover of logic and science. When her mother inherits a summer home on Selkie Island, Miranda arrives with no interest in the local legends of merfolk and sea creatures. As she sets about helping her mother dispose of the old home, she is drawn into a relationship with Leo, a boy who works at the marine center and who also possesses some very merman-like traits.

Lasky, Kathryn
Hannah. Daughters of the Sea, 1. 2009, Scholastic Press, ISBN: 9780439783101, 310p.

There are not many options for a 15-year-old orphan in 1899 Boston, so Hannah takes a job as a scullery maid for a wealthy family. Hannah is different—she leaves behind salt in the bathtub and feels sick when she is too far from the sea. When Mr. Wheeler arrives to paint a portrait of the wealthy family's daughters, he is able to see Hannah's special gifts. It is through Mr. Wheeler's interest that Hannah begins to piece together her identity.

Madigan, L. K.
The Mermaid's Mirror. 2010, Houghton Mifflin, ISBN: 9780547194912, 316p.

Ever since Lena's father had a surfing accident, he won't allow her to learn the sport. This is horrible for 16-year-old Lena, since she is deeply drawn to the sea. Convinced she has seen a mermaid at Magic Crescent Cove, Lena defies her father and starts learning to surf. When she experiences her own accident and almost drowns, the mermaid saves her and gives her a golden key—but to what?

Nielson, Sheila A.
Forbidden Sea. 2010, Scholastic Press, ISBN: 9780545097345, 304p.

Ever since Adrianne's father died, life has been hard. She and her family live on Windwaithe Island, a place that harbors superstitions against merfolk. A near-tragedy marks Adrianne, who is continually summoned by the Windwaithe mermaid. The mermaid wants Adrianne to join her under the sea, in a beautiful world complete with a handsome mer-prince. Will she leave her family for a life of ease and beauty?

Porter, Sarah
Lost Voices. Lost Voices Trilogy, 1. 2011, Harcourt, ISBN: 9780547482507, 304p.
    Fourteen-year-old Luce lives in a small Alaskan fishing village, neglected and abused by an uncle who clearly resents her. When an accident plunges her into the icy sea, she does not die. Instead, a tribe of mermaids save her and transform her into one of their own. Luce's new life is all she has ever dreamed of, until she finds out the catch: mermaids lure seafarers to their deaths with their bewitching voices. And with her beautiful singing voice, Luce can rise through the mermaid ranks and be their queen.

The Book Is the Thing: Characters with a Literary Edge

Some people might say there's nothing more magical than what's between the pages of a book. For these characters, books hold magic, wonder, power, and danger.

Beddor, Frank
The Looking Glass Wars. 2006, Speak, ISBN: 0803731531, 358p.
    Alyss Heart is very young when her evil Aunt Redd murders her parents, the King and Queen of Hearts. She escapes Wonderland through the Pool of Tears and ends up in Victorian England, where she is adopted by the Liddell family. Though Alice gets Charles Dodgson to write down her story, soon her memories of Wonderland are totally repressed. Then royal bodyguard Hatter Madigan shows up for her.

Ende, Michael
▶ *The Neverending Story*. 1983, Doubleday, ISBN: 9780385176224, 396p.
    Overweight and lonely, Bastian Balthazar Bux steals a special book and hides out in the school attic to read it. There he falls into a story-within-a-story; a magical place called Fantastica is disappearing, and Bastian realizes that only he can save it, but does he have the courage?

Funke, Cornelia ♛
Inkheart. Inkheart Trilogy, 1. 2003, Scholastic, ISBN: 078073007998, 534p.
    Twelve-year-old Meggie and her bookbinder father get along just fine in their quiet life of reading. When a menacing man named Dustfinger shows up, everything changes. Meggie learns that her father can read characters out of books, and when she was three years old, he accidentally released Dustfinger and other malicious characters from a book called *Inkheart*. Now those evil

characters are after Meggie and her dad, so that they may never be locked up between the pages of a book again.

Mantchev, Lisa
Eyes Like Stars. Theatre Illuminata Trilogy, 1. 2009, Feiwel and Friends, ISBN: 9780312380960, 356p.

Orphaned Bertie has been raised in the Theatre Illuminata, a place whose plays are governed by a magical book called The Complete Works of the Stage. Now 17, Beatrice has caused one too many problems, and she must prove her worth to the theater or leave forever. Beatrice decides to put on the best performance of Hamlet ever and return the theater to its glory, but is thwarted when one of the eternal actresses steals the book.

Scott, Michael
The Alchemyst. The Secrets of the Immortal Nicholas Flamel, 1. 2007, Delacorte Press, ISBN: 9780385733571, 400p.

Fifteen-year-old twins Sophie and Josh plan on having a low-key summer in their hometown of San Francisco. Josh is working at a bookstore owned by Nick and Perry Fleming when they are attacked by dead-looking creatures. The creatures are in search of the Codex, an ancient book containing the formulas for everlasting life. Soon Sophie and Josh are swept up in a centuries-old feud between alchemists John Dee and Nicholas Flamel.

Shulman, Polly ♛
The Grimm Legacy. 2010, G. P. Putnam's Sons, ISBN: 9780399250965, 336p.

Elizabeth is lonely at her New York private school, so when a teacher recommends that she take a job at the New York Circulating Material Repository, she jumps at the chance. She soon discovers that this is no ordinary library; there historical and fantastical items are housed, such as the Grimm Collection. When some of the more powerful artifacts begin to disappear, Elizabeth and her coworkers find themselves on a dangerous adventure.

Tooth and Nail: Animal Kingdoms

If you're in the mood for something completely different, try one of these anthropomorphic stories. Can you imagine a world where animals talk, dress, and think like humans, even develop entire civilizations complete with laws, customs, and wars? Makes you think twice about sweet little Rover lying at your feet, doesn't it?

Clement-Davies, David
The Sight. 2002, Dutton Books, ISBN: 9780525467236, 465p.

In medieval Transylvania, a pack of wolves flee from violent humans and an evil pack leader, Morgra. Their cubs are part of a prophecy of the Sight, a power that allows a wolf to see into the past and future and control minds. Larka grows into the Sight, but her loving pack is marked for death by Morgra and she has to watch them die one by one. As the young wolf sets out on her own, she must deal with the harsh environment and controlling her power for the greater good.

Hunter, Eric

The Quest Begins. Seekers, 1. 2008, HarperCollins, ISBN: 9780060871222, 293p.

An orphaned polar bear (Kallik), a captive black bear (Lusa), and a rebellious grizzly bear (Toklo), all leave their lives behind as they are beckoned by the Northern Lights. As they journey, the bears meet and realize they are on a special sort of journey, part of which is to escort a shape-shifting bear named Ujurak.

Jacques, Brian

Redwall. Redwall, 1. 1986, Philomel Books, ISBN: 9780399214240, 351p.

In a medieval-like colony of mice called Redwall Abbey, peace is threatened by the arrival of evil rat Cluny and his clan. Legend says the only thing that can save the Abbey is the lost sword of Martin the Warrior, and shy novice Matthias takes up the quest.

Lasky, Kathryn

▶ *Lone Wolf. Wolves of the Beyond, 1.* 2010, Scholastic Press, ISBN: 9780545093101, 240p.

Because of the mysterious mark on his deformed paw, baby wolf Faolan is abandoned by his pack. Doomed to die in the elements, he is saved and cared for by Thunderheart, a bereft mother bear. When tragedy befalls Thunderheart, Faolan is forced to seek out his own kind and fulfill the destiny for which he has been marked.

Paver, Michelle

Wolf Brother. Chronicles of Ancient Darkness, 1. 2005, HarperCollins, ISBN: 9780060728274, 295p.

Torak is 12 when he witnesses his father's death by a giant, demon-possessed bear. Vowing to take revenge and to save other clans from such attacks, Torak meets a wolf cub, and the two are able to communicate. Wolf becomes Torak's guide on his journey to the Mountain of the World Spirit, where Torak hopes to find the necessary spiritual and physical tools to defeat the demon.

Stewart, Sharon

Raven Quest. 2005, Carolrhoda Books, ISBN: 9781575058948, 320p.

Tok, a young and agile raven, is wrongly accused of murder, banished from his community, and stripped of his father's name. To redeem himself, Tok searches for the Grey Lords, legendary ancients who are crucial for the ravens' survival. He undergoes a harrowing journey and makes some unexpected alliances.

Bless Your Thieving Heart: Criminals

Crime doesn't pay, usually. But sometimes a pickpocket's talents or a computer hacker's skills can truly pay off. Check out these lovable lawbreakers.

Black, Holly ♛
The White Cat. Curse Workers, 1. 2010, Margaret K. McElderry Books, ISBN: 9781416963967, 320p.

Three years ago Cassel murdered Lila, his best friend. He doesn't understand how or why, but he *does* know that his family is curse workers: they are able to manipulate luck and emotion. Curse working is illegal, but Cassel learns his brothers have done it on him to carry out their scheme and to erase his memories. Once he learns the truth, Cassel must rely on his conman nature to save his name.

Bunce, Elizabeth C. ♛
Starcrossed. 2010, Arthur A. Levine Books, ISBN: 9780545136051, 368p.

As a street thief, 16-year-old Digger keeps her head down, but when her partner in crime gets killed, she goes on the run. After taking up with aristocrats, Digger lands a job as wealthy Meri's companion and is soon blackmailed into spying on the family she works for. Complicating it all are the flashes of magic Digger can see around Meri, and she learns of a rebellion against the intolerant government.

Colfer, Eoin
Artemis Fowl. Artemis Fowl, 1. 2001, Talk Miramax Books/Hyperion Books for Children, ISBN: 9780786808014, 277p.

Twelve-year-old Artemis is not only a genius, but he also comes from a criminal family. In fact, his father, Artemis Senior, lost the family fortune when a scheme against the Russian mob went awry. Now Artemis has a plan to win back that fortune—he will steal fairy gold and steal the magical book that contains all the fairies' secrets. Things heat up when Artemis kidnaps a mouthy elf by the name of Holly Short—and incites the wrath of the LEPrecon Unit.

Jinks, Catherine
▶ *Evil Genius.* 2007, Harcourt, ISBN: 9780152059880, 486p.

Cadel Piggott is not only a computer-hacking genius, but at age 13, he's already studying infiltration, misinformation, and embezzlement at the Axis Institute for World Domination. Cadel has been groomed for a life of crime by his mastermind father (who is in jail), but as time passes, he starts to question his values and wonders if he can break away.

Lackey, Mercedes
Take a Thief: A Novel of Valdemar. 2001, DAW Books, Inc., ISBN: 9780756400088, 351p.

Skif is an orphan who has the misfortune of living with his curmudgeon uncle. To make ends meet, he falls in with a gang of pickpockets, where he excels at crime. When one of the realm's magical horses chooses him, however, he must give up everything and become a servant of the queen.

Walden, Mark
H.I.V.E.: The Higher Institute of Villainous Education, 1. 2007, Simon & Schuster, ISBN: 9781416935711, 320p.

Thirteen-year-old Otto and three of his friends—geniuses all—are kidnapped and taken to H.I.V.E., a secret academy that trains supervillains. The H.I.V.E. is located atop a volcanic island, and escape is nearly impossible, but Otto and his friends scheme a way to get out. They will have a variety of obstacles to face, such as a flesh-eating plant, an omniscient computer, and a superior Ninja.

What's up, Bro? Sensational Siblings

You can choose your friends, as the saying goes, but not your family—especially your snotty little sister or obnoxious older brother. And sometimes, that's a good thing.

Kerr, Philip
The Akhenaten Adventure. Children of the Lamp, 1. 2004, Orchard Books, ISBN: 9780439670197, 383p.

A routine wisdom-teeth extraction leads to twins John and Phillipa's discovery that they are descended from a long line of djinn. They visit their Uncle Nimrod in London to learn more, but are being hunted by Iblis, an enemy djinn tribe who think they know the location of the powerful lost tomb of Akhenaten.

Patterson, James
Witch and Wizard. Witch & Wizard, 1. 2009, Little, Brown, ISBN: 9780316036245, 314p.

One night, Wisty and her brother Whit are roused from their sleep by the New Order and arrested on charges of witchcraft and wizardry. The siblings think such a charge is crazy until Wisty's powers manifest themselves in jail. They escape and hook up with a teen resistance determined to fight the corrupt government.

Riordan, Rick
▶ *The Red Pyramid. Kane Chronicles, 1.* 2010, Hyperion Books for Children, ISBN: 9781423113386, 516p.

Sadie and her older brother Carter have been separated since their mother's death; she lives in London with her grandmother; he travels the world with their Egyptologist father. They all get together for a reunion on Christmas Eve, but Sadie and Carter don't count on their dad unleashing the evil god Set at the British Museum. Their dad is entombed but the siblings escape, and they embark on a journey to not only save him but to understand the powers they have awakened in themselves.

Springer, Nancy
I Am Morgan le Fay: A Tale from Camelot. 2001, Philomel Books, ISBN: 0399234519, 227p.

Young Morgan resents her mother, who seems to prefer her half-brother Arthur. Left to her own devices, Morgan recognizes and accepts her powers, that of Fay, and struggles to control them. As her passions get the best of her, she realizes that she alone can bring down her half-brother Arthur and take his throne.

Williams, Maiya
The Golden Hour. Golden Hour, 1. 2004, Harry N. Abrams, ISBN: 0810948230, 259p.

Thirteen-year-old Rowan and his younger sister Nina are still grieving over the death of their mother when their father sends them to live with friends in Maine. The siblings make fast friends with twins Xanthe and Xavier, and they all explore an old resort hotel. The hotel is actually a time-travel portal, and offers adventures during the golden hour, the short time between day and night. Their adventures become more urgent when Nina disappears.

Wrede, Patricia C.
The Thirteenth Child. Frontier Magic, 1. 2009, Scholastic Press, ISBN: 9780545033428, 344p.

In an alternative Wild West, Eff is considered the unlucky 13th child to her twin brother Lan, the lucky and magical 7th son of a 7th son. The family has settled near the Great Barrier in order to hide the children's magical abilities, but Lan is found out when he uses magic against another student. After Lan is sent away, Eff is free to discover her own talents and her own identity.

Space Invaders: Aliens

Ever felt a little different from everybody else, perhaps even *alien*? Are you attracted to someone who doesn't quite seem like they're from this planet? These characters have been there, done that.

Ghislain, Gary
How I Stole Johnny Depp's Alien Girlfriend. 2011, Chronicle Books, ISBN: 9780811874601, 208p.

At age 14, David is used to his psychologist dad's weird patients. Zelda is exotic, beautiful, and claims she is an alien from the planet Vahalal, on a mission to find her soul mate, Johnny Depp. Somehow, David becomes Zelda's guide, all along hoping he can sway her feelings from the studly actor to himself. With only hours to succeed in her mission, Zelda drags David all over Europe, and they try to avoid other Vahalalians with the same intent.

Lewis, J. S.
Invasion. C.H.A.O.S. Novels, 1. 2011, Thomas Nelson, ISBN: 9781595547538, 320p.

After his parents are killed in a suspicious car wreck, 16-year-old Colt goes to live with his World War II–veteran grandfather in Arizona. As time goes by, Colt realizes that his memory has been erased, and he learns that his parents were murdered for investigating Trident, a company specializing in biotechnology. What ensues are a secret war involving aliens, comic book heroes and villains, and help from an organization known as C.H.A.O.S.

Logue, Mary ♛
▶ *Dancing with an Alien.* 2000, HarperCollins, ISBN: 9780060283186, 134p.

Branko is an alien whose planet is devoid of females, and he has been sent to earth to procure a female for breeding purposes. He finds that female when she rescues him from drowning—17-year-old Tonia has never met anyone like Branko before, and the two fall in love. When she learns his identity and purpose, they both must make some hard decisions.

Lore, Pittacus
I Am Number Four. Lorien Legacies, 1. 2010, Harper, ISBN: 9780061969553, 440p.

War forced nine alien children to flee their home planet of Lorien with their adult mentors. They have been hiding on earth ever since, waiting for their powers, or legacies, to develop. When they are in possession of these powers, they will return to Lorien to fight the evil Mogadarians. The Nine can only be killed in order, and Number Three is dead. Number Four is John Smith, so he and his father escape to a new town, where he waits for his powers to manifest, and he falls in love.

Mackel, Kathy
Alien in a Bottle. 2004, HarperCollins, ISBN: 9780060292812, 194p.

Eighth-grade Sean dreams of being a glass blower, but his parents won't support such a ridiculous dream. To attend a fine arts high school, Sean hopes to win a scholarship at the high school, so he is on the hunt for the perfect piece of glass. What he finds is a strange bottle in a dumpster, one that appears to be holding an entire spacecraft inside. The captain of the spacecraft is Tagg Orion, who has problems of his own.

Yansky, Brian
Alien Invasion and Other Inconveniences. 2010, Candlewick Press, ISBN: 9780763643843, 240p.

Aliens conquer earth and kill off most of humanity. The ones with telepathic abilities are spared, as they make excellent slaves. Jesse is one of these slaves, and as he struggles with his new existence, his telepathic powers grow. When he teams up with three other groups, they realize that their combined abilities might allow them to escape and find the rebel force out west.

Chapter Three

Setting

When people read for pleasure, often their primary desire is to escape, whether into a richly imagined magical forest or into the limelight of a juicy celebrity story in a gossip magazine.

For many spec lit readers, the setting, or world-building, of a story is of greatest importance. They want to be swallowed whole into completely alien societies, to live (vicariously) with nonhuman creatures, or to feel themselves shuttling millions of light years into space.

The following lists feature novels with prominent settings of all types and time periods, peopled by humans and nonhumans alike. Dive in and disappear for awhile, but be sure to drop a line when you get back.

School Sucks: Academies for the Extraordinary

At one time or another, most of us hated school, for whatever reason. Maybe our grades sucked, or we didn't get along with a teacher. Maybe the class bully beat us up for our milk money. Well, no matter how bad our school experiences were, nothing compares to the creepiness (and sometimes awesomeness) of these academies.

Armstrong, Kelly
  The Summoning. Darkest Powers, 1. 2008, HarperCollins, ISBN: 9780061662690, 390p.

When Chloe, aged 15, begins seeing ghosts, she is diagnosed as having schizophrenia and is sent to a group home called Lyle House. All along she has worried about her sanity, but once at Lyle House, she learns that her sanity is just fine—and her new friends have secrets.

Cast, P. C.

Marked. House of Night, Book 1. 2007, St. Martin's Griffin, ISBN: 9780312360269, 306p.

When Zoey Redbird turns 16, she becomes a fledgling vampire and enters the House of Night school to train. Not all fledglings survive the change, and complicating matters is the fact that vampire Goddess Nyx has marked her as special. Dealing with a new school and possible new powers ought to be enough, but then Zoey discovers the leader of the club Dark Daughters is abusing her gift—should Zoey stop her?

Gray, Claudia

Evernight. Evernight Series. 2008, HarperTeen, ISBN: 9780061284397, 310p.

The only good thing about 16-year-old Bianca's elite new school, Evernight Academy, is Lucas, who—like her—is an outsider. The Evernight type means you are gifted, rich, and beautiful, adjectives that, in Bianca's opinion, don't apply to her. Lucas is determined to find out the secret behind the academy, while Bianca harbors one of her own, and it just might unravel their romance.

Hawkins, Rachel

▶ *Hex Hall. Hex Hall Novels, 1.* 2010, Disney/Hyperion Books, ISBN: 9781423121305, 323p.

Sophie's always had magical abilities, but when a well-meaning spell goes horribly wrong at the prom, she is sent off to reform school. But Hex Hall is not just any reform school; it's a place for wayward Prodigium—kids with all manner of supernatural powers. As she tries to understand her background and learn how to control her abilities, Sophie finds herself in the middle of a murder mystery—something akin to a vampire is draining the popular girls and leaving them for dead.

Holder, Nancy

Possessions. 2009, Razorbill, ISBN: 9781595142559, 295p.

Lindsay Cavanaugh had such a rough time at her last school, she had an emotional breakdown, so when she wins a scholarship to Marlwood Academy, she hopes to start fresh. Then she learns the richest girl in school, Mandy, is possessed by an evil force and is luring others to her side. Lindsay snaps out of her depressed haze and tries to save as many of her schoolmates as she can.

Lockwood, Cara

Wuthering High. Bard Academy, 1. 2006, MTV, ISBN: 1416524754, 272p.

After some particularly bad behavior, 15-year-old Mia is shipped off to boarding school, the Bard Academy, known for treating troubled kids. Mia is not exactly looking forward to this change, and things get worse when she realizes all the teachers are ghosts—famous authors like Virginia Woolf and Ernest Hemingway who are stuck in limbo. Not all of the instructors are happy with their fates—Mia and her friends find themselves trying to stop an evil plan to take down the entire student body.

Mead, Richelle
Vampire Academy. Vampire Academy, 1. 2007, Razorbill, ISBN: 9781595143587, 332p.

> After being on the run for two years, Lissa (a human vampire princess) and her protector and best friend, Rose (half human, half vampire), are caught and returned to St. Vladimir's Academy. St. Vladimir's is like any other private school, except the way you handle gossip, cliques, and rumors can get you killed. On top of all that, evil forces called the Strigoi want to destroy Lissa.

Shields, Gillian
Immortal. Immortal series, 1. 2009, Katherine Tegen Books, ISBN: 9780061375804, 360p.

> Evie's dad is off in the military and her beloved grandmother has fallen ill, so Evie is shipped off to the Wyldcliffe Abbey School for Young Ladies. Evie cringes at the thought of attending boarding school with a bunch of snotty rich girls, but she is cheered by the attractive Sebastian, who lives somewhere on school grounds. When Evie starts to have strange visions, the truth about Sebastian comes to light.

Hipsters, Jokesters, and Monsters in the Subway: Urban Fantasy

Urban fantasy is where water sprites live in public drinking fountains, and elves bearing crossbows fight wars in the grocery store parking lot. The fey live right under the noses of humans and often seduce them into their realms. Try any of these titles, but don't eat anything from the fey courts—unless you plan to stay forever.

Armstrong, Kelly
The Gathering. Darkness Rising, 1. 2011, Harper, ISBN: 9780061797026, 400p.

> When she was 15, Maya's friend Serena unexpectedly drowned and Maya was unable to save her. Still feeling guilt over this a year later, Maya starts seeing cougars around her home in Salmon Island, but she doesn't fear them. Soon she realizes there's a connection between her paw-shaped birthmark, her deep love for animals, and the new bad boy in town, Rafe.

Black, Holly
▶ *Tithe: A Modern Fairy Tale.* 2002, Simon and Schuster, ISBN: 0689849249, 310p.

When Kay was little, she spent a lot of time playing with faeries. At age 16, she has just moved to New Jersey with her less-than-dependable mother and encounters Roiben. Roiben is tall, mysterious, and a Black Knight of the Unseelie Court. Suddenly, Kaye is caught up in a war between faerie realms, where her playmates from childhood want to sacrifice her—turn her into a tithe—to earn them seven years of freedom.

Caine, Rachel
Glass Houses. Morganville Vampires, 1. 2006, NAL Jam Books, ISBN: 9780451219947, 247p.

Sixteen-year-old Claire is a genius, a trait that gets her advanced placement at Texas Prairie University. There she is picked on by the popular cliques, but something much worse is going on in the town of Morganville—vampires and vampire hunters are at war. Soon Claire is in the thick of it all, doing anything to protect her friends.

Chadda, Sarwat
The Devil's Kiss. Devil's Kiss, 1. 2009, Disney/Hyperion Books, ISBN: 9781423119999, 327p.

Billi SanGreal has spent all her 15 years knowing she was a descendent of the Knights Templar, and she has been raised to hunt and kill the Unholy. And there are plenty of Unholy monsters out there trying to kill all the mortal inhabitants of London. Billi just wants to be a normal teen and hopes to break away from her fanatical father, but when a dark evil is unleashed, she has no choice but to fight.

Livingston, Leslie
Wondrous Strange. 2009, HarperTeen, ISBN: 9780061575372, 327p.

Seventeen-year-old Kelley Winslow gets to play the part of Titania in a production of A Midsummer Night's Dream when the lead actress is injured. She attracts the attention of Sonny Flannery, a changeling who guards the portal between the mortal and faerie realms. The two develop an attraction for one another, and Sonny begins to suspect that Kelley has fey blood. Kelley interacts with all sorts of otherworldly creatures, and she and Sonny are drawn into a major fey battle—all set in New York City.

Marr, Melissa
Wicked Lovely. 2007, HarperTeen, ISBN: 9780061214653, 328p.

Aislinn knows the rules: even though she has always been able to see faeries, she never lets them know. Having this ability is a curse, because most of the fey Aislinn encounters are cruel, vicious creatures intent on harming humans. Soon Aislinn realizes she is being pursued by one of them—the beautiful Summer King—who is determined to make her his queen.

White, Kiersten
Paranormalcy. Paranormalcy Trilogy, 1. 2010, HarperTeen, ISBN: 9780061985843, 335p.

Sixteen-year-old Evie has the ability to see supernatural creatures through their glamour. This attracts the attention of the International Paranormal Containment Agency (IPCA), an organization who tracks and controls all manner of monsters. Soon, Evie is enlisted by the IPCA and is steadily working for them when she finds herself attracted to Lend, a male shape-shifter her own age. When startling truths are revealed about the agency, Evie must make some hard decisions.

You Slay Me: Medieval Fantasy

There's something mystical about medieval times, the period when the Roman Empire fell and Europe was plunged into chaos. From the rampaging Germanic tribes, to the religious superstitions, to the old Pagan ways, Medieval Fantasy rises. The following titles encompass all that chaos, and more.

Black, Kat
A Templar's Apprentice. The Book of Tormod, 1. 2009, Scholastic, ISBN: 9780545056540, 288p.

Tormod is a bored farm boy in 14th-century Scotland, but his longing for adventure is granted when he meets Alexander, a member of the Knights Templar. Tormod has long suppressed his prophetic visions, but when he becomes Alexander's apprentice, he welcomes his powers, for the adventure Tormod has craved turns dangerous and he needs all the help he can get.

Dahme, Joanna
The Plague. 2009, Running Press Book, ISBN: 9780762433445, 272p.

Because orphan Nell so closely resembles Princess Joan, King Edward III enlists her to act as his royal daughter's body double. Nell travels with the royal party to Spain, where Princess Joan is to be married, but she falls dead under the plague. Her evil brother, the Black Prince, tries to force Nell to take his sister's place in a plot to overthrow the king, and Nell finds herself on the run through plague-ridden country.

Dunkle, Clare B.
By These Ten Bones. 2005, Henry Holt, ISBN: 9780805074963, 229p.

Maddie lives in a small, superstitious village in Scotland, so it's only natural that her people don't take too kindly to strangers Ned and his mute companion, young Paul. Maddie learns that Paul is a werewolf, contained from killing on full moon nights only by being chained down. The only way to save Paul, Maddie learns, is to offer herself as a sacrifice—something she willingly undertakes, with unexpected results.

McKenzie, Nancy
Guinevere's Gift. Chrysalis Queen Quartet, 1. 2008, Alfred A. Knopf, ISBN: 9780375843457, 327p.

Thirteen-year-old Guinevere has a gift with horses and is the center of a prophecy claiming she will be queen of the land. This is not likely, since she is an orphan, living with her royal aunt and uncle. When the men go off to war and her cousin Elaine is kidnapped, Gwen relies on her tomboyish nature, her wits, and her gifts with animals to rescue Elaine and the castle.

Rallison, Janette
My Fair Godmother. 2009, Walker & Co., ISBN: 9780802797803, 320p.

When sophomore Savannah loses her boyfriend to her perfect older sister, she fervently wishes for a Cinderella-like life, one complete with a ball, gown, and charming prince. Enter an aspiring fairy godmother, Chrissy, who is not quite in control of her magic, and Savannah finds herself transported to the Middle Ages.

Thesman, Jen
▶ *Singer.* 2005, Viking, ISBN: 9780670059379, 304p.

Twelve-year-old Gwenore escapes her covetous and evil witch mother, Rhiamon, and takes refuge for many years in the countryside, learning the arts of healing, singing, and nurturing the magical powers symbolized by a birthmark on her wrist. She becomes the beloved teacher of the children of magical king Lir, and all is well until her mother returns to wreak havoc.

Yo Ho Ho! Nautical Fantasy

Ah, the sea. Some of the world's greatest adventures happen on the sea, and the stories in this list take adventure even further—sharks, pirates, vampires, time travel—what's not to love? *Yargh!*

Frazier, Angie
Everlasting. 2010, Scholastic Press, ISBN: 9780545114738, 329p.

It's 1855, and 17-year-old motherless Camille has four months of freedom left before she is married to her captain father's business partner. She decides to spend those months on her father's ship as it travels from San Francisco to Australia, but a storm sinks the ship. With only the sailor Oscar to accompany her, Camille makes her way to Australia, where she learns her mother is alive and holds the key to a magical stone.

Meyer, Kai
Pirate Curse. Wave Walkers, 1. 2006, Margaret K. McElderry Books, ISBN: 9781416924210, 336p.

Fourteen-year-old Jolly is an orphan raised by pirates and she is a polliwog—someone who can literally walk on water. Jolly loves her seafaring life until her adoptive father and his crew are betrayed. Jolly escapes and ends up on an island, where she meets Munk, another polliwog. According to the mysterious Ghost Trader, Jolly and Munk are the only ones who can stop the return of an evil named Maelstrom.

Plum-Ucci, Carol
The She. 2003, Harcourt, ISBN: 9780152168193, 280p.
> Evan has lost his parents in a freighter accident. What's worse is that Evan heard the whole thing over ship-to-shore communication, along with the unearthly shrieking of the legendary sea monster The She. Evan's older brother won't even entertain thoughts of the supernatural, but Evan meets Grey, a girl who claims to have also heard The She. The teens begin to investigate and are faced with the question: is The She a real, supernatural force? Or were Evan's parents killed by drug runners?

Somper, Justin
Vampirates: Demons of the Ocean. Vampirates, 1. 2006, Little, Brown, ISBN: 9780316013734, 336p.
> Fourteen-year-old twins Connor and Grace have grown up listening to their dad's creepy stories of an ancient ship that haunts the oceans. When he dies, the siblings are left with nothing, so they run away to sea. A storm separates them; Connor is rescued by pirates, while Grace is taken aboard the Vampirates—the very ancient ship of their dad's stories.

Vaughn, Carrie
▶ *Steel.* 2011, HarperTeen, ISBN: 9780061547911, 304p.
> Jill, an accomplished fencer, loses a match that would've sent her to the Junior World Fencing Championships. To escape her disappointment, she joins her family on a Caribbean vacation. When she finds the tip of an old rusty rapier, she doesn't realize she has picked up a piece of magic until she is transported back in time—to an 18th-century pirate ship. Her fencing skills serve her well as she fights her way back home.

Ward, James M.
Midshipwizard Halcyon Blithe. Halcyon Blithe Fantasies, 1. 2005, Tor, ISBN: 9780765312532, 288p.
> Halcyon Blithe is descended from a long line of magically skilled officers in the Arcanian navy, so when he turns 16, he enlists on the Sanguine. The Sanguine is a vessel built on the back of an actual dragon, and Halcyon, along with other magical recruits, must learn to sail this half-vessel, half beast, as well as fight a shape-shifting enemy called the Maleen.

The Far East: Stories Set in Asia— or Something Like It

For many of us, just the mention of the Far East conjures up images of a magical land, full of colors and spices and ancient mysticism. Whether you want ninjas or Indian goddesses, these novels won't disappoint.

Banker, Ashok
Prince of Ayodhya. Ramayana, 1. 2003, Warner Books, ISBN: 9780446530927, 387p.

In ancient India, a seer foretells of an attack on the peaceful city of Ayodhya by a great demon lord. It is up to teenage prince Rama and his reluctant half-brother Lakshman, to set out on a perilous journey that pits absolute good against horrific evil.

Jordan, Devin
The Dragon's Pearl. Adventures of Marco Polo, 1. 2009, Simon & Schuster Books for Young Readers, ISBN: 9781416964100, 352p.

Marco Polo is 16, living in Venice with his grandfather and waiting for his father to return home from his adventures in the east. When his father vanishes, Marco and his friend Amelio undertake the voyage east themselves, traveling through the Unknown Lands and beyond the mountains. Once there, Marco and Amelio descend on the Peking court of Kublai Khan for answers.

Lake, Nick
Blood Ninja. Blood Ninja Trilogy, 1. 2009, Simon & Schuster, ISBN: 9781416986270, 369p.

In 16th-century Japan, the powerful samurais are also vampires—which is a good thing. After young Taro is mortally wounded by a ninja attack, a vampire samurai saves him and also turns him into a member of the undead. Soon Taro begins training for his destiny—he just may be the one to end a deadly feud between mighty warlords ruling the country.

Pon, Cindy
▶ *Silver Phoenix: Beyond the Kingdom of Xia.* 2009, Greenwillow Books, ISBN: 9780061730214, 338p.

Ai Ling is sure the gods have more in store for her than just marrying the sinister Master Huang. When her father travels to the emperor's palace and doesn't return, Ai Ling has found her destiny. She is determined to travel to the palace and rescue her father herself, and also put an end to an evil council advisor who stays unnaturally alive by feeding off the souls of others.

Stone, Jeff
Tiger. Five Ancestors, 1. 2005, Random House, ISBN: 9780375830716, 224p.

In 1650 China, five orphans live in a Buddhist monastery, learning to hone their martial arts skills under the tutelage of the Grandmaster. Each boy has an animal name that most resembles their personality; Fu (Tiger) is brash and impetuous. After a raid on the monastery leaves the Grandmaster dead, Fu rescues the sacred scrolls and flees, seeking vengeance from a former brother known as Eagle.

Tomlinson, Heather ♛
Toads and Diamonds. 2010, Henry Holt, ISBN: 9780805089684, 288p.

In the precolonial Hundred Kingdom of India, two sisters are blessed (or cursed) with very different powers: Diribani produces gems and flowers when she speaks, and Tana spits out snakes and frogs. While Diribani is revered in the royal court, Tana is chased out of the village. But the bond between the girls is strong and Tana returns in disguise—for her curse might just turn out to save the kingdom.

Follow That Dirigible! Steampunk

Nothing is more cool than steampunk—alternative history where steam machines are the prime mode of power. Time is all mashed up in steampunk fiction, where futuristic devices work alongside steam engine trains, all handled by characters wearing really awesome Victorian clothes.

Clare, Cassandra
Clockwork Angel. Infernal Devices, 1. 2010, Margaret K. McElderry Books, ISBN: 9781416975861, 496p.
Sixteen-year-old Tessa is searching for her missing brother, which leads her to Victorian-era London. There she is kidnapped by the Dark Sisters, who force her to develop an unrealized supernatural power to shape-shift. She is rescued from the Dark Sisters by the Shadowhunters, young demon hunters, who decide to help Tessa find her brother and reveal the identity of the nefarious Magister. (This series is a companion to Clare's Mortal Instrument books.)

Colfer, Eoin ♛
▶ *Airman.* 2008, Hyperion Books for Children, ISBN: 9781423107507, 416p.
Set in the 19th century, 14-year-old Conor Broekhart was born in a hot-air balloon and feels best when he is in the air. Then a conspiracy lands him in a brutal prison, where he must mine for diamonds. Conor knows he cannot survive the prison much longer and designs a flying machine, but escape will take all his wits and the help of his friends.

Dolamore, Jaclyn
Magic under Glass. 2010, Bloomsbury's Children's Books, ISBN: 9781599904306, 225p.
When her family falls into disgrace, Nimira, once wealthy, finds herself out on the streets looking for work. When an attractive sorcerer named Parry offers her a job—he wants her to sing accompaniment with his life-size piano-playing automaton—she moves into his grand house. Then odd, haunting things start to happen and Nimira wonders if she made the wrong choice.

Opel, Kenneth ♛
Airborn. Airborn Adventures, 1. 2004, Eos, ISBN: 9780060531805, 368p.
Matt Cruse is a cabin boy aboard the luxury airship Aurora. His peaceful life in the skies is interrupted by the arrival of an old man and his granddaughter,

Kate, who come aboard from a decrepit hot-air balloon. The old man reveals he has seen beautiful winged creatures flying over an island. Soon, pirates attack, the Aurora crash lands on an island, and Matt and Kate are caught up trying to prove the existence of the winged creatures.

Pullman, Philip ♛
The Golden Compass. His Dark Materials, 1. 1995, A. A. Knopf, ISBN: 9780679879244, 399p.

In an alternate London, Lyra and her daemon Pan, roam the halls of Jordan College in Oxford, where she is a ward of the Scholars. Always ready for a fight or an adventure, Lyra spies on a meeting organized by her Uncle Asriel and learns about the mysterious Dust located in the Arctic. Meanwhile, children are being kidnapped by Gobblers; a strange woman named Mrs. Coulter appears, and Lyra acquires a golden compass that can answer questions to the person who knows how to read it.

Slade, Arthur ♛
The Hunchback Assignments. Hunchback Assignments, 1. 2009, Wendy Lamb Books, ISBN: 9780385737845, 278p.

Though 13-year-old Modo is a hunchback, his shape-shifting abilities allow him to change his appearance any way he likes. He is saved from a traveling sideshow by Mr. Socrates, who enlists him in the Permanent Association, a secret group that defends Victorian England from the evil machinations of the Clockwork Guild. Modo eagerly joins the group but wonders if he is prepared for all the dangerous adventures ahead of him.

Westerfeld, Scott ♛
Leviathan. Leviathan Series, 1. 2009, Simon Pulse, ISBN: 9781416971733, 440p.

During an alternate World War II, the world is divided by two opposing forces: the Darwinists, who genetically manipulate animals, and the Clankers, who create terrible machines. Deryn Sharp disguised herself as a boy in order to enlist, and her bravery lands her aboard the living airship Leviathan. Meanwhile, Prince Alek, son of Archduke Ferdinand, is on the run after his parents are murdered. Alek and Deryn collide in the Swiss Alps and combine forces to survive.

Fight the System! Corrupt Societies

These characters have to deal with a lot more than just curfews and driver's permits. Try having your skin sanded off or your essence removed. The governments in these novels are up to no good; mostly everybody is brainwashed except those bright few who stand out—and stand up.

Condie, Allyson Braithwaite ♛
Matched. 2010, Dutton Children's Books, ISBN: 9780525423645, 369p.

The Society is perfect—it chooses everything for its citizens, education, careers, even spouses. Cassia is living contentedly, sure in the knowledge that her match is Xander, a boy she has known since childhood. But then a new face is thrown into the mix—Ky, a boy from the Outer Provinces—and Cassia can't stop thinking about him. As she begins to think for herself, Cassia realizes that the Society is not as perfect as it claims to be.

DeStefano, Lauren

Wither. Chemical Garden, 1. 2011, Simon & Schuster Books for Young Readers, ISBN: 9781442409057, 368p.

Twenty-first-century American science created one generation of perfect babies, without illness or handicap. It also unleashed a virus that kills young men off at age 25, young woman at age 20. Rhine is 16 and has been kidnapped to serve as a breeder in a polygamous marriage with a wealthy man. In hopes of escape, Rhine climbs the ranks until she is First Wife and obtains the freedom necessary to run.

Doctorow, Cory ♛

Little Brother. 2008, Tor Teen, ISBN: 9780765319852, 384p.

In a future San Francisco, the Department of Homeland Security has taken ultimate control. Seventeen-year-old Marcus picks the wrong day to cut school; he's caught near the sight of a terrorist attack. Six days of brutal inter-rogation follows, and when he is released, Marcus decides to use his computer hacking skills to fight back.

Fukui, Isamu

Truancy. 2008, Tor Teen, ISBN: 9780765317674m, 431p.

In the City, control is obtained through an oppressive education system. This doesn't sit well for many students, and some have formed a resistance group called the Truants. When 15-year-old Tack's sister is killed in a violent resistance attack, he joins the Truants seeking to get close to their leader and take his revenge. But some of the group's philosophy rings true for him, and he finds himself torn between helping himself or the greater good.

O'Brien, Caragh ♛

Birthmarked. 2010, Roaring Book Press, ISBN: 9781596435698, 368p.

Lake Michigan dried up 300 years earlier, but 16-year-old Gaia has no need for this history. She is busy living in Western Sector Three, helping her midwife mother deliver their monthly quota of three infants to the Enclave. Gaia has never questioned her way of life, until her parents are suddenly ar-rested and marked for execution. Springing into action, Gaia sneaks into the Enclave to rescue her parents and to discover for herself the truth about their existence.

Singer, Nicky

Gem X. 2008, Holiday House, ISBN: 9780823421084, 311p.

In the future, there are two kinds of people: the rich and genetically enhanced and the Dreggies, those who have had no enhancements. Sixteen-year-old Maxo is a product of GemX, the best in genetic engineering, and he is perfect in every way. Then, out of nowhere, a crack appears in his face. Others in his generation who have undergone the GemX treatment are also cracking, and as he digs deeper, Maxo not only falls for a Dreggie girl, but he uncovers a conspiracy.

Westerfeld, Scott
▶ *Uglies. Uglies, 1.* 2005, Simon Pulse, ISBN: 9780689865381, 448p.

When they turn 16, Tally Youngblood and her best friends will all undergo radical surgery to make them Pretties. Not only will they be gorgeous, but they will also cross the river and live a bubbly party life. Tally is looking forward to the day when she will no longer be an Ugly, but then her friend Shay runs off and ruins it all. Evil Dr. Cable forces her to retrieve Shay from the hidden Smoke settlement, or never be Pretty at all.

But It Looks Like Home: Parallel Universes

Ever get that strange déjà vu feeling, as though you'd done something before, or been in a certain place before? Maybe you have...maybe you just glimpsed a hole in the fabric of an alternate universe. Try out a few of these titles and see if you're right.

Becker, Tom
Darkside: Book 1. 2008, Orchard Books, ISBN: 9780545037396, 232p.

Fourteen-year-old Jonathan's father is locked up again, having gone into another one of his fits about a secret world called Darkside. Jonathan thinks it's all nonsense until the vicious kidnappers begin to stalk him. He escapes to the very world his father always raved—Darkside—a horrific 17th-century world beneath modern London. In Darkside, Jonathan navigates monsters and other dangers, all the while searching for a cure that will save his father.

Gaiman, Neil ♛
Coraline. 2002, HarperCollins, ISBN: 9780380977789, 162p.

Bored and feeling neglected by her parents, Coraline ventures through a mysterious door in her new flat and finds a very similar world. This world is populated by her other mother and father, creatures who look just like her parents but who have black buttons in place of eyes. Coraline finds every pleasure in the other world, until things get creepy—her other mother wants her to stay forever, and won't let Coraline escape.

Hoffman, Mary
▶ *Stravaganza: City of Masks. Stravaganza, 1.* 2002, Bloomsbury, ISBN: 9781582347912, 344p.

In modern-day London, Lucien is undergoing chemotherapy, which leaves him depressed and weak. A mysterious book allows him to slip into an alternate 16th-century Venice-like city called Bellezza. Lucien renames himself "Luciano" and feels his vibrancy for life return in the beautiful city. He meets Ariana and Rodolfo, who has created the book that is a talisman—a stravagation—that allows Luciano to travel between worlds. His happiness, however, is disrupted when he runs afoul of the Duchessa who rules Bellezza.

Kellerman, Kaye
Prism. 2009, Harper, ISBN: 9780061687211, 264p.

A car wreck leads 15-year-old Kaida and two schoolmates to seek refuge in a desert cave, and all three are instantly transported to an alternate dimension. This new place looks exactly like the world they left behind—complete with school and families. The only difference is, medicine and health care are forbidden, and if someone becomes ill, they usually are expected to die. Kaida is suddenly involved with rebel Ozzy and the dangerous underworld of drug trafficking.

MacHale, D. J.
The Merchant of Death. Pendragon, 1. 2002, Aladdin, ISBN: 9780743437318, 375p.

Bobby Pendragon is popular, talented, and smart—everything a normal 14-year-old could want. His normal world is turned upside down when Uncle Bobby comes to visit and reveals that Bobby is a Traveler—someone who can move through time. It isn't long before Bobby travels to a strange medieval land, where the Milago are enslaved by the ruling Bedoowan. As it turns out, Bobby must free the Milago, relying on other Travelers and a girl named Loor.

Meyer, Kai
Water Mirror. Dark Reflections, 1. 2005, Margaret K. McElderry Books, ISBN: 9780689877872, 256p.

In an alternate Venice, supernatural elements are commonplace: stone lions can fly, and mermaids swim in the canals. Orphans Junipa (who is blind) and Merle become apprentices to a magical mirror maker. The city has been threatened by Egypt for 36 years; the only thing keeping it safe was the power of the Flowing Queen. When the girls discover the queen has been captured, Merle sets off on a quest to save the city.

Shinn, Sharon 🏆
Gateway. 2009, Viking, ISBN: 9780670011780, 288p.

Adopted Chinese American Daiyu buys a ring from a woman on the streets of St. Louis, then walks through the Arch and is instantly transported in time to an alternate America. In this universe, the Chinese have settled the West and are the ruling class, leaving whites and blacks as the minority. Daiyu is soon swept up in racial and class struggles, wondering who to trust and how to get back home.

Smith, Andrew ♛
The Marbury Lens. 2010, Feiwel and Friends, ISBN: 9780312613426, 368p.

Sixteen-year-old Jack is kidnapped after a drunken night, but he manages to escape. He tells no one of the incident except for his best friend, Connor. The two arrive in London for a summer break, as planned, and a stranger hands Jack a pair of glasses. When Jack wears the glasses, he can see another world called Marbury. In Marbury, there is war, cannibalism, and despair. When Connor also appears in Marbury as a murderer, Jack wonders if he has lost his mind.

Give Me Space: Exploring the Universe(s)

Supposedly space is the final frontier, the last unexplored wild in the universe. We humans dream about space travel, and wonder, and wait. Grab any of these novels, strap yourself in, and get ready for a long ride.

Card, Orson Scott
Pathfinder. Pathfinder, 1. 2010, Simon Pulse, ISBN: 9781416991762, 432p.

Thirteen-year-old Rigg has always helped his trapper father, but he has been educated as well. When his father dies, Rigg sets off to find the sister he has never known somewhere in the capital city. Aiding Rigg is his ability to see the paths of all living things, through time and space. Accompanying him on the journey is his friend Umbo, who has a gift of his own, and together they stumble across friends and enemies.

Haarsma, P. J.
Virus on Orbis 1. Softwire, 1. 2006, Candlewick, ISBN: 9780763627096, 272p.

JT has spent his 12 years growing up on the spaceship Renaissance. He, his sister, and 198 other orphans are heading to the Rings of Orbis. Once they arrive on Orbis 1, the children learn they will be slaves to the alien Guarantors to pay off their passage. JT is a softwire, someone who can communicate with computers. When the computer that controls Orbis begins to fail, the aliens suspect JT, and he must prove his innocence.

Ness, Patrick ♛
The Knife of Never Letting Go. Chaos Walking, 1. 2008, Candlewick Press, ISBN: 9780763639310, 492p.

Todd Hewitt is the only boy living on an alien planet full of men. A virus has killed all the women and infected the men with a strange ability to broadcast all their thoughts, all the time. Todd is constantly surrounded by Noise. When he discovers Viola—the first girl he has ever seen—he is suddenly targeted by a zealot preacher and must flee.

Osterlund, Anne
▶ *Academy 7.* 2009, Speak, ISBN: 9780142414378, 259p.

After six traumatic years as a slave on an alien planet, 17-year-old Aerin Renning has escaped and been accepted at Academy 7, an exclusive military school. Soon her arch nemesis emerges in the form of Dane Madousin, the rich, cocky son of a powerful Alliance member. Both discover top secret government information, and coupled with a budding attraction, the two decide to work together.

Revis, Beth
Across the Universe. 2011, Razorbill, ISBN: 9781595143976, 400p.

Sixteen-year-old Amy and her parents undergo cryogenic suspension on the starship Godspeed, with the intention of being awakened 300 years later on an alien planet. Amy awakens 50 years early to find a plague has wiped out most of the inhabitants of the starship, and there is evidence that someone has tried to murder her. As Amy investigates, she meets another teen, Elder, who is training to be leader, but together they begin to uncover lies, deceit, and deadly secrets.

Tests, Dom
The Comet's Curse. Galahad, 1. 2009, Tor Teen, ISBN: 9780765321077, 240p.

Two hundred years into the future, a comet blows past earth and leaves behind a deadly disease that kills all adults. Children are immune to the plague, but only for a limited time—once they grow up, they will also succumb to the illness. Hoping to save the human race on another planet, scientists send 251 teens into space; 16-year-old Triana is their leader and captain. Things are already tense onboard the ship when an adult is discovered—one that is potentially carrying the disease.

The New Normal: Future Life

Once upon a time, people laughed at the idea of handheld computers, streaming video, and music that could be downloaded onto tiny portable machines. You never know what might happen in the future, but these novels make great guesses.

Anderson, M. T. ♛
Feed. 2002, Candlewick Press, ISBN: 9780763617264, 237p.

Titus and his friends live on an earth ravaged by global warming, yet they travel to the moon for spring break. They also have the Feed implanted in their heads—an instant connection to media and advertising that can almost predict what people want before they want it. Nobody reads or writes, and everybody is self-absorbed, except for Violet, who longs for a life of free thinking and creativity. When a hacker takes down the Feed, Titus has to think for himself for the first time—and he sees another side to life.

Bacigalupi, Paolo ♈
Ship Breaker. 2010, Little, Brown, ISBN: 9780316056212, 326p.

    In a post-global warming world, 15-year-old Nailer lives on the Gulf Coast, scavenging copper off grounded oil tankers to make a meager living. His father is a violent drug addict, and life is bleak until he discovers a modern clipper ship washed up on the beach. Convinced all the copper from this ship will make him rich, Nailer does not expect to find an injured girl aboard. Does he abandon his plans, or does he save the girl?

Falls, Kat
Dark Life. 2010, Scholastic Press, ISBN: 9780545178143, 304p.

    Climate changes have destroyed most of the Earth's surface, and people can either live Topside, piled together in cramped apartments, or live below the water on the ocean floor. Ty is 16 and has lived his entire life on the ocean floor—a Dark life; he cares little for Topsiders until he meets Gemma, an orphan who is searching for her lost brother. Ty agrees to help, but they run afoul of the vicious Seablite pirates.

Fisher, Catherine ♈
Incarceron. 2010, Dial Books, ISBN: 9780803733961, 442p.

    Finn can't remember a life outside Incarceron, a vast, cruel, sentient prison, but he knows he comes from somewhere else. Life in the prison is brutal; no one ever gets out or in. Finn hopes to change his luck when he finds a crystal key that can open any door. Outside Incarceron, the warden's daughter, Claudia, is looking for a way in to escape an arranged marriage; she, too, has a crystal key. The two meet and agree to help each other, no matter how high the stakes.

Hauge, Lesley
Nomansland. 2010, Henry Holt, ISBN: 9780805090642, 256p.

    Society as we know it is long gone. Keller is a young tracker-in-training for a tribe of women who live without men, vanity, or interpersonal relationships. Keller feels something is missing in her life; she and the other trackers-in-training come upon an old house from the Time Before, where they discover makeup, magazines, and clothing. This opens Keller's eyes to what life used to be like, and what it could possibly be now.

Reeve, Phillip ♈
Mortal Engines. Hungry City Chronicles, 1. 2003, HarperCollins, ISBN: 9780060082079, 310p.

    In the future, entire cities have gone mobile and constantly move over earth's destroyed surface. The larger cities consume the smaller ones for their power and materials. On London's Traction City, 15-year-old Tom is apprenticed to Head Historian, Valentine; after an attack, Valentine purposely pushes Tom off the city. Tom survives, and along with Hester and two other teens, he tries to get back to the City and uncover a conspiracy.

Shusterman, Neal 🏆

▶ *Unwind.* 2007, Simon & Schuster Books for Young Readers, ISBN: 9781416912040, 335p.

After the Second Civil War, kids between the ages of 13 and 16 can be unwound by their parents and their organs harvested to the highest bidder. When 16-year-old Connor learns his parents plan to have him unwound, he runs away from his Ohio home, where he meets and teams up with two other Unwinds.

Smith, Alexander Gordon

Lockdown. Escape from Furnace, 1. 2009, Farrar, Straus, and Giroux, ISBN: 9780374324919, 273p.

The law has cracked down with an iron fist on juvenile criminals; in fact they have built a brutal prison deep underground and controlled by super-beings. Alex is sentenced to life in this prison after being framed for murder; he and his fellow inmates must race to their cells whenever a siren sounds (lockdown) or face death. One day, Alex catches the smell of fresh air near his work zone and becomes obsessed with escaping.

It's About Time...Travel

Like wormholes? Find yourself thinking about a fifth dimension? Ever wonder what would happen if you could go backward—or forward—in time? Wonder no more! These stories cover it all.

Bell, Ted

Nick of Time. Nick McIver Time Adventure, 1. 2008, St. Martin's Griffin, ISBN: 9780312380687, 434p.

Twelve-year-old Nick McIver lives on an island in the English Channel; one day he finds a sea chest on the shore, and inside is a time machine, along with a request for help from an 18th-century ancestor. So begins Nick's time-traveling adventures as he bounces back and forth fighting pirates, Napoleon's naval forces, and Nazis in 1939. Alongside all this, Nick undertakes a quest to save two wealthy children from Billy Blood, a pirate with a time machine of his own.

Bloor, Edward

▶ *London Calling.* 2006, Alfred A. Knopf, ISBN: 978037583650, 304p.

Martin has started seventh grade at a prestigious prep school, but his class-mates constantly remind him that he is a scholarship kid. When he begins work on an at-home project, he fiddles with an old radio and is suddenly transported back in time, to World War II and the London Blitz. There Martin meets Jimmy, a boy in the Blitz who has an urgent message.

Buckley, Linda Archer

Gideon the Cutpurse: Being the First Part of the Gideon Trilogy. 2006, Aladdin, ISBN: 9781416915256, 416p.

Peter and his new friend Kate stumble across an antigravity machine in 21st-century London and are whisked back in time to the year 1763. Before they can even register what is happening, Peter and Kate lose the machine to the Tar Man, London's most infamous criminal. Luckily they meet Gideon, a reformed thief who agrees to help them return home.

Bush, Penelope

Alice in Time. 2011, Holiday House, ISBN: 9780823423293, 196p.

Fourteen-year-old Alice Watkins's life is a mess: she can't believe her mother left her father; her little brother is a demon, and a bully torments her at school. A merry-go-round accident somehow sends her back in time to her seven-year-old self, where she gains new perspective on certain issues and sees where she can make different choices to affect her future.

Cockcroft, Jason

Counter Clockwise. 2009, Katherine Tegen Books, ISBN: 9780061255557, 202p.

Nathan's world is turned upside down when his mother dies in a bus accident. Nathan's estranged and somewhat odd father decides he will prevent his wife's death by any means necessary—and that means traveling back in time to stop the accident. Soon Nathan is caught up in the time-travel whirlwind, chasing his father over and over again to the time of his mother's accident and living out various alternative futures.

Curry, Jane Louise

The Black Canary. 2005, Margaret K. McElderry Books, ISBN: 9780689864780, 288p.

James is a biracial child of two musicians and feels no desire to follow in their footsteps. Angry and resentful, he finds a portal in a London flat and is carried back 400 years to Elizabethan times. Once in this time period, James finds that his beautiful singing voice and his biracial skin garner him much favor with the Queen. He begins to perform with the Children of the Royal Chapel and is so swept up in his new life that he wonders if he should stay there forever.

Klass, David ♛

Firestorm. Caretaker Trilogy, 1. 2006, Frances Foster Books, ISBN: 9780374323073, 304p.

Senior Jack Danielson becomes an instant star on the football team after his speed and agility win a new record. But his sudden fame draws the attention of sinister forces, and his father sends him away with vague warnings that everything he's ever known is a lie. Soon Jack learns he has been sent back in time to stop global warming, but the evil Dark Army has come back with him, determined to stop him at all costs.

Chapter Four

Mood

When the leaves begin to change color, signaling autumn (and Halloween), do you crave terror? Having a bad week (or month, or year) and just need a laugh? Sometimes nothing but ghost stories will do. Other times you long for a good, bloody fight, albeit from the sidelines.

Mood is all about making the reader feel something—grossed-out, creep-tastic, intrigued, or mystified. Often speculative fiction is just what the doctor ordered, since mood tends to just ooze from these stories. Look for your favorite squeal-inducing topics here, or tiptoe into unknown horrors. You won't be sorry...*Muah ha ha ha ha ha!*

I See Through You: Ghostly Encounters

Chances are, someone you know has seen a ghost. Maybe they've even spoken to or done a favor for one. Or been pursued and haunted relentlessly by one. Whatever the case, ghostly visitors are sure to give you a chill no matter what they want.

Archer, Jennifer
Through Her Eyes. 2011, HarperTeen, ISBN: 9780061834585, 240p.

Tansy Piper's mom is a famous horror author, and she has become used to moving all over whenever Mom starts a new project. This time they've landed in her grandfather's hometown, dusty little Cedar Canyon, Texas, in a reputedly haunted house. A passionate photographer, Tansy begins seeing through her camera lens people and scenes from World War II. Is she going crazy, or is Henry, the boy she sees through the camera, really a trapped ghost in need of help?

Cabot, Meg

Shadowland. Mediator, 1. 2005, Avon Books, ISBN: 9780060725112, 245p.

Sixteen-year-old Suze Simon is a mediator, a person who helps ghosts resolve their issues so they can move on. When her mother remarries, moving them to California, Suze hopes to start afresh. But then an attractive ghost from the 19th century shows up in her bedroom, and his revenge-seeking dead ex-girlfriend gets angry.

Gaiman, Neil ♛

▶ *The Graveyard Book.* 2008, HarperCollins, ISBN: 9780060530921, 312p.

As a toddler, Nobody Owens escapes a brutal attack that leaves the rest of his family dead. The ghosts in the local cemetery take on the responsibility of raising him, along with Silas, Nobody's mysterious otherworldly guardian. As Nobody grows up, he longs for the world beyond the cemetery, but danger lies outside in the form of a man named Jack.

Jenkins, A. M.

Beating Heart: A Ghost Story. 2006, HarperCollins, ISBN: 9780060546076, 244p.

After his parents divorce, 17-year-old Evan moves to an old Victorian house with his mother and little sister. With his mother distracted by remodeling, Evan is left to his own devices and discovers a box of files and photos hidden in the walls. The box reveals a girl named Cora, who lived in the house 100 years earlier and who is still there. What's more, she's developed a powerful crush on Evan.

Marsh, Katherine ♛

The Night Tourist. 2007, Hyperion Books for Children, ISBN: 9781423106890, 232p.

Jack is only a freshman in high school, but he is a classics prodigy. Still grieving the loss of his mother, Jack buries himself more and more in the ancient stories. When he is struck by a car, Jack finds that he is physically uninjured but now he can see ghosts. In the New York subway system he meets Euri, a ghostly girl who leads him below Grand Central Station where hundreds of other dead beings reside. Can Jack find his dead mother here and bring her back?

Morris, Paula

Ruined: A Ghost Story. 2009, Scholastic, ISBN: 9780545042154, 309p.

When 15-year-old Rebecca's father must travel overseas, she is sent to live in New Orleans with an eccentric aunt. Having grown up in bustling New York, Rebecca is not prepared for the strange societal customs and snobbery of her new classmates. The situation worsens when she meets Lisette, a ghost who resides in the cemetery across from her aunt's home. Lisette died under mysterious circumstances, and as Rebecca tries to uncover details, she finds herself swept up in old curses, voodoo, and much more.

Naylor, Phyllis Reynolds

Jade Green: A Ghost Story. 2000, Atheneum, ISBN: 9780689820052, 168p.

When Judith becomes an orphan at 15, she is taken in by an elderly uncle in South Carolina. Her uncle is kind but tells her she cannot bring anything green into the house. As Judith adjusts to her new life and makes friends, she is troubled by her creepy adult cousin, Charles, and ghostly happenings in the house. Then she learns of a girl named Jade Green, who also lived in the house but died a horrific death. Jade is trying to tell Judith something— but what?

Schroeder, Lisa

I Heart You, You Haunt Me. 2008, Simon Pulse, ISBN: 9781416955207, 226p.

Ava is 15 and has never experienced the loss of anyone she loves until her boyfriend Jackson dies in a car wreck. When Jackson shows up as a ghost, Ava is at first thrilled. But as she works through her grief and finds herself ready to move on with her life, she doesn't know how to tell Jackson.

Slime Included: Monsters

Dracula. The Swamp Thing. Frankenstein. Everybody's heard about these monsters, but what about the others—the unknown ones? Well, they were unknown until they crept up into these stories.

Allende, Isabel

City of the Beasts. Alexander Cold Trilogy, 1. 2002, HarperCollins, ISBN: 9780060509187, 416p.

While Alex's mother battles with cancer, he is shunted out of his California home and onto a wild adventure with his grandmother, Kate, a writer for International Geographic. Her assignment is to locate the giant Bigfoot-like creatures roaming in the Amazon, known only as Beasts. As Alex and company travel up the Amazon River, he becomes friends with the guide's mystical daughter, never expecting what is to come next.

McNamee, Graham 🏆

Bonechiller. 2008, Wendy Lamb Books, ISBN: 9780385908955, 294p.

Danny's mother has died, sending him to live with his estranged father in a tiny frozen Canadian town. When Danny is stung by a giant, horrible creature, he gets more and more sick and relentlessly dreams about the monster. Danny's new girlfriend Ash, who is part Ojibwa, tells him the legend of the Windigo, a beast with a taste for human flesh. Since the police won't help, it's up to Danny and his friends to hunt the Windigo down, but they are racing against time.

Reeves, Dia
Bleeding Violet. 2010, Simon Pulse, ISBN: 9781416986188, 454p.

Sixteen-year-old Hannah is a black Finnish girl with manic depression. She flees an aunt who wants her back in a mental institution and finds the mother she's never known in Portero, Texas. Her mother uneasily agrees to take her in, which should make Hannah happy—except for all the demons roaming around. When she meets Wyatt, a demon killer, she joins him on his mission to stop an ancient evil.

Richards, Justin
The Death Collector. 2006, Bloomsbury Children's Books, ISBN: 9781582347219, 336p.

Eddie is a street urchin roaming the foggy streets of Victorian London. His path crosses with two other teens, George and Liz, and they all become involved in the death of a museum clerk. As it turns out, a crazed inventor known as Mr. Lorimore has plans to reanimate the dead—both human and dinosaur—for wretched purposes.

Wooding, Chris
Malice. 2009, Scholastic Press, ISBN: 9780545160438, 384p.

An urban legend says that if you call for creepy Tall Jake six times and burn special ingredients, he will whisk you off to a horrific realm called Malice. Seth and Kady scoff at the legend, because really, it's all just a part of a comic book. But then their friend Luke vanishes, and a character who looks just like him appears in the comic strip. Seth and Kady realize the legend is true and decide to venture into the world of Malice to save Luke.

Yancy, Rick 🏆
▶ *The Monstrumologist. Monstrumologist, 1.* 2009, Simon & Schuster Books for Young Readers, ISBN: 9781416984481, 434p.

It's 1888 and young Will Henry is an apprentice to New England scientist Dr. Warthrop. Warthrop hunts down and studies monsters, and Will diligently records all their findings. The newest danger in town is the Anthropophagi, huge, headless beasts who eat human flesh. Amidst guts, gore, and grave robbers, Will and the doctor search for a way to stop the beasts.

Yovanoff, Brenna 🏆
The Replacement. 2010, Razorbill, ISBN: 9781595143372, 343p.

Sixteen-year-old Mackie Doyle knows that he is a changeling; every seven years in his town, a human baby is swapped with a replacement from the creatures who live underground, thus protecting the town's prosperity. But now

Mackie is severely ill, and when a new baby is stolen, he is drawn into the chaotic world of the changeling clans.

It Was a Dark and Stormy Night: Gothic Fantasy

Sometimes Gothic fiction takes place in the steamy, creepy old South, among the ruins of antebellum homes and overgrown bougainvillea. Other times, these stories of the macabre happen in completely normal settings—like your own backyard.

Berk, Ari

Death Watch. Undertaken Trilogy, 1. 2011, Simon & Schuster Books for Young Readers, ISBN: 9781416991151, 496p.

When Silas Umber's mortician father disappears, Silas and his mother move into his uncle's mansion, in a town full of ghosts and secrets. To escape his mother's alcoholism and his uncle's weirdness, Silas explores the town and comes to know the many spirits haunting the town. He even begins to embrace his destiny as an undertaker, one who assists souls in moving on to the next realm.

Clement-Moore, Rosemary

The Splendor Falls. 2009, Delacorte Press, ISBN: 9780385906357, 300p.

Sylvie was a promising ballerina until a broken leg shattered her career. When her father dies and her mother remarries, Sylvie's grief gets worse and worse. Finally, she is sent from Manhattan to Alabama, to live with an extended family in a home that is being restored. Once there, Sylvie learns more than she ever wanted to know about her family history, and she also finds herself caught up in a love triangle.

Garcia, Kami

Beautiful Creatures. Caster Chronicles, 1. 2009, Little, Brown Books for Young Readers, ISBN: 9780316042673, 576p.

Sixteen-year-old Ethan can't wait to get out of his small South Carolina town where nothing changes. When new girl Lena shows up, his whole world is rocked: they are psychically linked. Lena comes from a family of spell casters, and getting close to her lets Ethan time travel, witness supernatural events, and fall deeply into love.

Golds, Cassandra

▶ *In the Museum of Mary Child.* 2009, Kane/Miller Book Publishers, ISBN: 9781935279136, 329p.

Heloise lives with her rigid godmother, who has raised her without toys, books, or love. Heloise has learned to escape into her imagination, until one day she discovers a doll. Though she tries to keep the doll secret, her godmother finds out and drags her next door, to the creepy Museum of Mary Child. Once in the museum, Heloise learns a shocking truth—not to mention her meeting with the defaced museum dolls who come to life.

Marlowe, Paul
Sporeville. Wellborn Conspiracy, 1. 2007, Sybertooth, ISBN: 9780973950540, 215p.

Fifteen-year-old Elliot is a very logical and scientific teen. He doesn't understand why, after the death of his mother, his father moves them to a boring little fishing town called Sporeville. Things continue to get strange is Sporeville, like the sleepwalker townspeople, all the fresh graves, and a girl named Paisley who has especially sharp teeth. When Elliot catches his father sleepwalking, he concludes that something evil is afoot and begins the scientific business of uncovering what it is.

Priestly, Chris
Mr. Creecher. 2011, Bloomsbury Children's Books, ISBN: 9781599907031, 250p.

In 19th-century London, 15-year-old Billy is an orphan and a pickpocket, and this is how he makes his living. Then he meets Mr. Creecher, a terrifying giant of a man, who takes Billy under his protection. Soon Billy finds himself along for the ride as Creecher tracks down two men—one of them named Frankenstein.

Trent, Tiffany
In the Serpent's Coils. Hallowmere, 1. 2007, Mirrorstone, ISBN: 9780786942299, 291p.

Sixteen-year-old Corrine has been plagued by dreams of faeries who seem to be warning her of impending doom. When her parents are killed in the Civil War, Corrine is sent to Falston Manor in Virginia, where she hopes she can find some peace. This is not to be, for just as other girls begin disappearing from the school, Corrine's dreams come back with a vengeance.

Stranger with My Face: Possession

Nothing is creepier than possession. *Nothing.* Just imagine another being—more often than not a malicious one—taking up residence in your body. You're shoved back into your own subconscious while the possessed part of yourself takes over and wreaks havoc. Pick up one of these novels and see how others deal with it.

Alender, Katie
Bad Girls Don't Die. 2009, Disney/Hyperion Books, ISBN: 9781423108764, 346p.

Alexis doesn't fit in—and she's glad. Flaunting her outside status, she often skips school to take and develop pictures. It is through this medium that she starts to notice strange things about their house—spheres of green light, faulty air conditioning, the creepy basement. When her little sister Kasey's behavior grows more erratic, Alexis makes a discovery—Kasey is demon-possessed.

Holt, Simon
▶ *The Devouring.* 2008, Little, Brown, ISBN: 9780316035736, 231p.
Reggie works at a bookstore and loves horror novels. When she finds a strange journal in a box of used books, she takes it home and reads about the Vours, smokelike demons who feed on fear and take over one's body. Reggie and her friend Aaron jokingly summon a Vour, leading to disaster—the demon takes over the body of her timid little brother Henry.

Showalter, Gena
Intertwined. 2009, Harlequin Teen, ISBN: 9780373210022, 440p.
Aden Stone is not only an orphan living on a ranch for troubled boys, he's also possessed by four different souls. Each soul inside his head has a different supernatural power, such as foretelling the future and traveling into the past, and each day is a battle for Aden. All Aden wants is to free himself and have a normal life. When he meets Mary Ann, she can neutralize the voices, and he thinks he might be on the road to normal at last.

Singer, Nicky
The Innocent's Story. 2007, Holiday House, ISBN: 9780823420827, 220p.
In England, 13-year-old Cassina Dixon and her little sister are killed by a terrorist bombing in a music store. Cassina is then transformed into a para-spirit—a mist cloud that can enter the minds and bodies of a variety of hosts. As she comes to terms with her death, Cassina inadvertently enters the head of the terrorist and discovers where his next target will be.

Springer, Nancy
Possessing Jesse. 2010, Holiday House, ISBN: 9780823422593, 96p.
Jessie's brother, Josh, was shallow and reckless; while street racing the family car, he crashed into a tree and died. Now Jessie's mother is so grief-stricken she doesn't even acknowledge Jessie's presence. Jessie begins to wear Josh's clothes, talk and even walk like him. As time passes, Jessie realizes she is no longer just pretending to be Josh—Josh is possessing her, in want of his life back.

Whitcomb, Laura ♛
A Certain Slant of Light. 2005, Graphia, ISBN: 9780618585328, 282p.
Helen has been dead for 130 years and unable to move on for reasons unknown. Her spirit survives by inhabiting a series of hosts—she prefers the literary kind—but not possessing them. When she meets James, she realizes

he is another spirit who has figured out how to inhabit a body. James instructs Helen how to do the same, and in their corporeal bodies, the two fall in love.

Shades of Fantasy: Magical Realism

Sometimes you want to escape from home but not wander too far. That's when you can reach for one of these novels. All deal with real-life people and situations, but there's a slight twinge of the magical or supernatural in each—just enough to make you look around and wonder, "What if?"

Antieau, Kim
Ruby's Imagine. 2008, Houghton Mifflin, ISBN: 9780618997671, 201p.

Ruby is 18, living in a ward of New Orleans with Grammaloose. She has a unique way of looking at the world—her imagine—where she communes with the trees and the birds and the insects. Butterflies warn her of a Big Spin, but Grammaloose has no patience for Ruby's imagination. But when Hurricane Katrina hits, it's Ruby's imagine that helps local people get through the disaster and to see hope.

Block, Francesca Lia ♛
Weetzie Bat. Weetzie Bat 1. 1999, Harper & Row, ISBN: 9780060205348, 88p.

Colorful flower child Weetzie Bat has never really been understood, not by her divorced parents or her high school peers. On a search to create a happy home in Hollywood, Weetzie and best friend Dirk go duck-hunting for their perfect mates. Dirk finds his Duck, while Weetzie finds her Secret Agent Lover Man. They all set up house together and begin to make underground movies—but when Weetzie finds out she is expecting, Secret Agent Lover Man disappears.

Bowler, Tim
Frozen Fire. 2008, Philomel Books, ISBN: 9780399250538, 272p.

Years ago, 15-year-old Dusty's brother told her, "Goodbye, Little Dusty," and disappeared from her life forever. When she gets a phone call from a strange boy who claims he has overdosed, he says the same exact words to her. Convinced this strange boy knows something about her missing brother, Dusty starts out into the snowy landscape, following his footsteps and searching for answers.

Dominguez Greene, Michelle
▶ *Chasing the Jaguar.* 2006, HarperCollins, ISBN: 9780060763534, 237p.

Right before she turns 15, Martika begins to have strange dreams about jungles and jaguars. She also has startling nightmares about a white rich girl who has been kidnapped. When Martika's mother takes her to the local *bruja* (witch), they discover Martika is descended from the *curanderas* (Mayan medicine women with special powers) and that her visions of the kidnapped girl are very much real.

Monninger, Joseph
Hippie Chick. Journey Trilogy, 1. 2008, Front Street, ISBN: 9781590785980, 156p.

Fifteen-year-old Lolly is an old hand at sailing, as she takes her boat out on the Florida Keys all the time. Then she capsizes and is injured. In a dreamlike state, she realizes she is being rescued by a trio of manatees, who tow her to an uninhabited island. As Lolly begins the long journey of healing, she relies on these gentle creatures, who commune with her and eventually tow her back home.

Sweeney, Joyce
Waiting for June. 2003, Cavendish Children's Books, ISBN: 9780761451389, 144p.

High school senior Sophie was never very popular, but she always dreamed of attending college. Now pregnant and even more isolated, she is still determined to get an education, as well as learn the identity of her own birth father. Meanwhile, she refuses to reveal her own baby's father and is content with the visions the baby sends to her in dreams—but someone is not so content with the situation and threatens to harm Sophie and the baby.

Charmed, I'm Sure: Fantasy Chick Lit

There are certain issues in life faced by all girls. How do I clear up my acne? Which pair of heels should I wear on Saturday? And how do I turn my best friend's jerk of a boyfriend into a toad? Grab one of these girl-exclusive novels for an enchanting beach read.

Benway, Robin
The Extraordinary Secrets of April, May, and June. 2010, Razorbill, ISBN: 9781595142863, 256p.

Life is already complicated for teen sisters April, May, and June: their parents have divorced; they've moved to a new town and started a new school; and now latent magical talents have surfaced in each of them. June can read minds, May can turn invisible, and April can predict the future. What April sees is alarming—a host of catastrophic events that involve family members.

Burgiss, Stephanie
Kat, Incorrigible. Unladylike Adventures of Kat Stephenson, 1. 2011, Atheneum Books for Young Readers, ISBN: 9781416994473, 304p.

In Regency England, when a young girl can't do much, Kat Stephenson discovers her magical abilities. This is both an exciting yet daunting development, since Kat has not yet learned to control her powers. What she hopes to do is save her older sister from a loveless marriage, while keeping the Order (a group who seeks her abilities) at bay.

Harrison, Lisi
Monster High. Monster High, 1. 2010, Little, Brown, ISBN: 9780316099189, 255p.
When you're created in a lab, chances of fitting in with normal society are slim, but this is Frankie Stein's biggest hope. When she enrolls in Mount Hood High School, all Frankie wants is to blend in with everyone else—but other students are not so sure she deserves the chance.

Johnson, Maureen ♛
▶ *Devilish.* 2006, Razorbill, ISBN: 9781595140609, 263p.
Senior Jane Jarvis is short and smart-mouthed and has a hard time dealing with the nuns at St. Theresa's Preparatory School for Girls. She's just broken up with her boyfriend, Elton, and her best friend Ally is acting completely out of character. When new student Lanalee reveals that she is a demon and that Ally has traded her soul for popularity, Jane is skeptical and even goes so far as to trade places with her best friend. That's when things get all too real.

Larbalestier, Justine
How To Ditch Your Fairy. 2008, Bloomsbury, ISBN: 9781599903019, 307p.
Fourteen-year-old Charlie lives in New Avalon, where everyone has a fairy who helps out in certain aspects of life. Charlie's best friend has a clothes-shopping fairy; her most hated enemy has an every-boy-will-love-you fairy. Meanwhile, Charlie is stuck with a parking fairy. Feeling she is cursed, Charlie tries everything to get rid of her fairy and attempts to find a better one.

Mlynowski, Sarah
Bras and Broomsticks. Magic in Manhattan, 1. 2005, Delacorte Press, ISBN: 9780385731812, 311p.
Rachel lives in New York City and is struggling to keep up with the popular crowd at school. When she discovers that both her mother and her little sister, Miri, are witches with fabulous magical powers, she is livid that she is not similarly gifted. Then she begins to make plans: can Miri help her get popular? Make boys notice her? Keep their divorced father from remarrying? The girls embark on all sorts of escapades and learn just how far magic can safely go.

Myracle, Lauren
Rhymes with Witches. 2005, Amulet Books, ISBN: 9780810958593, 207p.
Jane is a freshman at Crestview Academy and is, well, plain. She can't believe it when the school's most popular clique, The Bitches, ask her to join them. All she has to do is steal something from a classmate each week and leave it in the office of creepy teacher Lurl the Pearl. She can shake off her conscience for only so long until The Bitches viciously turn on a classmate. When Jane intervenes, it isn't long before she feels the wrath of the clique's black magic.

Don't Make Me Laugh: Humor

Who says speculative fiction has to be all doom and gloom, maniacal killer wizards, and slime-dripping aliens? Take a walk on the lighter side with these titles.

Archer, E.
Geek: A Fantasy Novel. 2011, Scholastic Press, ISBN: 9780545160407, 110p.
Fourteen-year-old Ralph Stevens and the British cousins he goes to visit all have magic in their families but have been forbidden by their parents to use it. The cousins talk each other into their hereditary right to make one wish—and when disaster ensues, they wish they hadn't!

Cottrell Boyce, Frank 🏆
▶ *Cosmic.* 2010, HarperCollins, ISBN: 9780061836862, 320p.
Poor Liam is a giant of a 12-year-old, complete with facial hair, and he's often expected to behave more maturely than he rightfully should. Sick of it all, he pretends to be a grown-up in a contest where the winner will chaperone a bunch of kids on a flight into space—and he wins! Suddenly Liam and the bunch he's chaperoning are 239,000 miles from home, with nothing but space—and other things—to keep them company.

Green, Lisa
The Secret Society of the Pink Crystal Ball. 2010, Sourcebooks Fire, ISBN: 9781402241062, 315p.
When Erin's beloved aunt dies, she is bequeathed a strange, pink crystal ball with a set of vague instructions. Erin is too preoccupied with winning a coveted trip to Italy with her AP history class to pay much attention to the crystal ball, not to mention a bully who is harassing her best friend. Then, on a whim, Erin starts to ask the crystal ball for predictions—and they start to come true with alarming results.

Lubar, David
Wizards of the Game. 2003, Philomel Books, ISBN: 9780399237065, 176p.
Eighth-grader Mercer's favorite role-playing game is Wizards of the Warrior World, where his alter ego is Shath'dra the Warrior Mage. After attempts to get his school to host a Wizards of the Warrior World tournament, a local minister whips up a frenzy of fear, claiming the game is evil and dangerous. Mercer thinks this belief is crazy—until four homeless guys start to follow him around and call him "Magus." Are these men really four lost wizards from another dimension?

Papademetriou, Lisa
The Wizard, the Witch, and Two Girls from Jersey. 2006, Razorbill, ISBN: 9781595140746, 288p.

Sophomores Veronica and Heather are complete opposites—Veronica is brainy and into fantasy; Heather is a fashionista and into nail polish—and they are assigned to write an English paper on the fantasy novel *The Queen of Twilight*. As the girls fight over a copy of the novel, they somehow fall into the story, and must follow the plotline in order to get back out again. Things go awry when Heather begins to deviate from the story's events.

Pratchett, Terry ♛
The Amazing Maurice and His Educated Rodents. Discworld (Young Adult) 1. 2002, HarperCollins, ISBN: 9780060012342, 241p.

Maurice, a scheming cat, and his friends, some very intelligent rats, talk a young musician named Keith into a heist: play the pipes and the rats will follow him out of various towns, after pillaging them for various benefits. The heists work perfectly until the educated rats start to feel guilty. They agree to pull off one more heist in the village of Bad Blintz, where a secret terror is lurking.

Rex, Adam
Fat Vampire: A Never Coming-of-Age Story. 2010, Balzer & Bray, ISBN: 9780061920905, 336p.

After being bitten by a vampire, 15-year-old overweight Doug is doomed to be unattractive for all eternity. Though Doug now gets terrible sunburn, he carries on with life as usual, going to school and Comic Con and trying to find willing sources of blood. He becomes enamored with Sejal, a new student from India, who unfortunately does not return his interest. On top of it all, Doug must take vampire lessons from a creepy old vamp in order to deal with his new powers.

Teague, Mark
The Doom Machine. 2009, Blue Sky Press, ISBN: 9780545151429, 376p.

Jack Creedle is a juvenile delinquent who comes from a family of brilliant criminals, namely his uncle Jack, who is a great inventor. Enter the Skeeps, a group of spiderlike aliens led by Commander Xaafuun, who covets Uncle Jack's dimensional field stabilizer. Jack, along with Isadora, the daughter of a local scientist, finds himself on a breakneck space adventure as they try to stave off the aliens.

Blood and Guts: Fantastic Gore

Maybe you're in the mood for some nitty-gritty, bone-cracking, teeth-shattering, monster demolition. Or perhaps blood-gushing horror is your cup of tea. If you're looking for flesh dripping off bones and rolling heads, pick any one of these titles.

Delaney, Joseph ♆
Revenge of the Witch. Last Apprentice, 1. 2005, Greenwillow Books, ISBN: 9780060766184, 344p.

    In a long-ago England, 12-year-old Tom is the seventh son of a seventh son and is apprenticed to the local Spook, whose job it is to keep the town safe from witches, bogarts, and other monsters. Tom faces flesh-rotting zombies and the gory staking of all manner of creatures and is getting along well—until he has to face Mother Malkin, a dangerous witch.

Higson, Charles
The Enemy. Enemy series, 1. 2010, Hyperion, ISBN: 9781423131755, 440p.

    In London, a flesh-eating plague has turned everyone over the age of 16 into zombies who stalk the unaffected. Groups of resourceful kids all over the city have holed up in places like grocery stores, but even venturing outside for a moment is life threatening. When a young messenger reveals that Buckingham Palace is a safe haven, Sam and his friends decide to undertake the harrowing journey.

Horowitz, Anthony
▶ *Raven's Gate. Gatekeepers, 1.* 2005, Scholastic Press, ISBN: 9780439679954, 254p.

    Because 14-year-old orphan Matt was involved in a robbery gone wrong, he is sent to a foster home in a remote, rural Yorkshire farm. It's no fun being under the strict supervision of Mrs. Deverill, but Matt realizes something worse is brewing in the nearby village of Lesser Malling. The villagers are planning to open Raven's Gate, an evil portal to another world, and they will employ all manner of violence to proceed with their goal.

Sedgwick, Marcus ♆
My Swordhand Is Singing. 2007, Wendy Lamb Books, ISBN: 9780375846892, 205p.

    In 17th-century Eastern Europe, wanderers Peter and his depressed, tortured father take work as woodcutters in a remote village. A grisly murder sets off rumors of walking dead, and soon, there is no doubt—recently deceased villagers are rising again in search of human flesh. A band of gypsies, complete with young princess Sofia, entreat Peter's father to unearth his hidden weapon—a silver sword—and put an end to the unholy killings.

Shan, Darren
Lord Loss. Demonata, 1. 2005, Little, Brown, ISBN: 9780316114998, 233p.

    After Grubbs Grady witnesses the brutal death of his entire family by an evil demon named Lord Loss, he lands in the country home of his strange uncle Dervish. Uncle Dervish reveals the long and bloody history of the family, including werewolves, and Grubbs finds himself a reluctant participant in his new macabre world.

Wooding, Chris ❦
The Haunting of Alaizabel Cray. 2004, Orchard Books, ISBN: 9780439598514, 304p.

In an alternate London, demonic *wych-kins* lurk in the dark, waiting to feed on unsuspecting humans. Thaniel Fox is a 17-year-old *wych*-hunter, fighting the creatures with means both magical and physical. When he finds a traumatized girl named Alaizabel, he learns that she escaped a cult known as the Fraternity, who deposited an evil spirit into her body.

Chapter Five

Language

Words are the building blocks of all writing. How often and how easily many of us overlook this very basic, yet integral, part of reading. In our fast-paced, lightning-speed society, we all learn the message that quicker is better. Sometimes this translates to readers' preferences, too.

However, we can't overlook readers whose first love is language, those who swoon over rich description and eloquent turns of phrase. Others delight in witty dialogue, distinctive tones, or up-close-and-personal narrators.

This chapter offers lists of high fantasy, snappy reads for the reluctant, top-rated audiobooks for MP3 addicts, and much more. Whether you are selecting graphic novels, classics, or intense, multivolumed sagas, there's something for every language lover out there.

Simply Delicious: Lyrical Fantasy

Here, fabulous worlds engulf you as luxuriously as the softest quilt settling over your shoulders. Images wind rich and sensuous through you. Characters choose their words carefully because they have nothing but the utmost respect for language. Think of these titles as the most sumptuous layer cake you've ever tasted. And then go back for seconds.

Block, Francesa Lia
The Waters and the Wild. 2009, HarperTeen, ISBN: 9780061452451, 128p.
When Bee turns 13, she meets her doppelganger who appears in her room one night. With the help of two eccentric friends who have identity issues of

their own, Bee discovers she is really a fairy who has been switched at birth. Before her doppelganger takes her life back, the three friends decide to make the most out of their lives. In this spare but poetic novel, Block makes every lovely word count.

Croggan, Allison
The Naming. The First Book of Pellinor. 2005, Candlewick Press, ISBN: 9780763626396, 492p.

Maerad is 16 and has only known life as a slave on a small mountain outpost. One day a man named Cadvan rescues her and sets her on her true path—Maerad is a Bard, prophesized as the One who will save the land of Edil-Amarandah from the dark Nameless One. Croggan's challenging read is deepened even more with her vivid descriptions.

Fisher, Catherine ♛
Corbenic. 2005, Greenwillow Books, ISBN: 9780060724702, 288p.

Seventeen-year-old Cal has put up with his mother's mental illness all his life. When a wealthy uncle offers to take him in, Cal jumps on a train, heading toward what he hopes will be normalcy. Instead he disembarks in an Arthurian Waster Land, finds a decrepit castle called Corbenic, and meets a crippled man named the Fisher King. What ensues is a grave error on Cal's part and his difficult journey to right his wrongs. Complex both stylistically and intellectually.

Gardner, Sally
▶ *I, Coriander.* 2005, Dial Books, ISBN: 9780803730991, 280p.

In 17th-century London, Coriander suffers at the hands of a cruel stepmother. Things change when she discovers her deceased mother was actually a fairy princess whose magical, silvery homeland needs Coriander's help. Coriander moves back and forth between England and the fairy kingdom, undergoing a quest that will not only save the magical world but also that of the humans. A lush, leisurely historical fantasy.

Larbalestier, Justine ♛
Magic or Madness. Magic or Madness Trilogy, 1. 2005, Razorbill, ISBN: 9781595140227, 288p.

For 15 years, Reason and her mother have been on the run from her grandmother, Esmeralda. Reason's mother has told her all sorts of terrible stories about her grandmother and her dark witchcraft. When her mother goes insane, Reason is sent to live with Esmeralda and sinks deeper into family lore, terrifying ritual, and portal travel. First in the series, this novel has been called hypnotic and fierce.

McKinley, Robin
Chalice. 2008, G. P. Putnam's Sons, ISBN: 9780399246760, 272p.

Mirasol is a quiet beekeeper who is summoned by the new Master of Willowlands to be the Chalice—a female charged with communicating with the land.

The former Master abused the land and devastated much of it, so Mirasol has her work cut out for her. Complicating matters is the prohibited attraction she feels for the new Master, who is no longer completely human. Intricate and layered.

Napoli, Donna Jo
The Wager. 2010, Henry Holt, ISBN: 9780805087819, 262p.

In 12th-century Italy, Don Giovanni loses everything in a flood and is forced to beg on the streets to survive. Desperate to return to his former stature, Don Giovanni makes a wager with the Devil—he agrees to stop bathing for three years in exchange for an endless supply of gold. As his physical appearance degenerates, Don Giovanni begins to experience an inner transformation. Rich and evocative.

Private Property: Diary Stories

You know it's wrong, but you can't stop yourself. You come across someone's journal, just lying there, waiting to reveal untold secrets and guilty pleasures alike. Dive into these diary stories and see what other's thoughts reveal.

Adlington, L. J. ♛
The Diary of Pelly D. 2005, Greenwillow Books, ISBN: 9780060766153, 282p.

On a futuristic colony, 14-year-old Toni is working on City Five, which has been devastated in the recent war. His drill hits a watering can, where a diary has been hidden. Toni sneaks the diary home and reads about its owner— Pelly D—a girl who was once rich and privileged. But genetic branding reveals that Pelly is from the undesirable Galrezi race, and she quickly falls from a life of privilege to misery—and worse.

Cary, Kate
Bloodline. Bloodline, 1. 2005, Razorbill, ISBN: 9781595140128, 324p.

Lieutenant John Shaw witnessed many horrible things during his time fighting the Great War in France—including his bloodthirsty captain, Quincey Harker. Things get worse when John's sister Lily falls in love with Captain Harker, who whisks Lily off to be married in Romania—in a creepy castle much like the one in Bram Stoker's *Dracula*.

Hale, Shannon ♛
Book of a Thousand Days. 2007, Bloomsbury Children's Books, ISBN: 9781599900513, 305p.

Fifteen-year-old Dashti is a maid who has sworn her allegiance to her mistress—even if that means sharing in Lady Saren's punishment. Because Saren has refused to marry a powerful suitor, she is to be locked in a dark tower for seven years, along with Dashti. Dashti records their trials and tribulations in a diary, and as time passes, their situation becomes grim: rats have eaten their food; Saren is slowly going mad, and enemies threaten to burn the tower with the girls still in it. Dashti knows they must escape, but how?

Haydon, Elizabeth
The Floating Island. Lost Journals of Ven Polypheme, 1. 2006, Starscape, ISBN: 9780765308672, 368p.

    In recently discovered journals, readers meet Ven, a 13-year-old boy from a sprawling, ship-building family. Ven can't seem to find his place in the family business and is on the newest cruiser when they are attacked by pirates. Using his wits, Ven defeats the pirates, and is thrust head-first into high adventure, including mermaids, fairies, ghosts, and an inn filled with evil.

Lloyd, Saci
▶ *The Carbon Diaries 2015.* 2009, Holiday House, ISBN: 9780823421909, 330p.

    Global warming has become so treacherous that England is the first country to ration carbon dioxide. Laura Brown is vexed by this—she just wants to use her cell phone and play guitar with her band. To cope, she documents the first year she and her family live with the rationing, as the elements continue to pummel the city with dramatic results.

Pfeffer, Susan Beth ♀
Life As We Knew It. 2008, Harcourt, ISBN: 9780152061548, 347p.

    An asteroid is predicted to hit the moon, but the event is supposed to be mild enough that 16-year-old Miranda and her family can watch it happen from the comfort of their front yard. No one is prepared for the tsunamis, earthquakes, and volcanoes that erupt all over the world. Life as Miranda knows it begins to collapse around her, and she details the struggle in her journal as things grow more and more dire. (See companion novels *The Dead and the Gone* and *This World We Live In.*)

Pierce, Tamora ♀
Terrier. Beka Cooper: 1. 2006, Random House Children's Books, ISBN: 037581468X, 581p.

    Sixteen-year-old Beka Cooper is an orphan and toughened from life in Tortall's slums. Her quest for justice and her magical gifts lead her to become a Puppy—a trainee with the Provost's Guard, or Dogs. Her first crimes are to solve some mysterious disappearances in the Lower City, and also the kidnapping and murder of children by something called the "Shadow Snake."

Time for Just One: Short Story Collections

When life is crazy and you have limited time, or when you just don't feel like getting attached to a novel, short story collections are perfect. You can dip in and out of all these anthologies, have a brief visit, and then be on your way.

Black, Holly and Larbalestier, Justine, Eds.
▶ *Zombies Vs. Unicorns.* 2010, Margaret K. McElderry Books, ISBN: 9781416989530, 256p.

Which side would win in an ultimate supernatural battle? These 12 short stories, offered by authors such as Libba Bray, Scott Westerfeld, and Carrie Ryan, all vie for the reader's vote. Read on to reveal the winner!

Cabot, Meg. (et al.)
Prom Nights from Hell. 2007, HarperTeen, ISBN: 9780061253096, 304p.

Everybody has a nightmarish tale about prom, but these five stories take the…tiara. Authors include Stephanie Meyer and Lauren Myracle, and they give us vampires chasing after prom queens, demons duking it out on the dance floor, and other scenarios that truly are hellish.

Datlow, Ellen and Windling, Terri, Eds.
The Faery Reel: Tales from the Twilight Realm. 2004, Viking, ISBN: 9780670059140, 528p.

Seventeen different authors reimagine the fey living in modern time: fairies who live in children's sandcastles; a goblin hiding as a man of the cloth; sprites stealing dreams—it's all here. Read a poem by Neil Gaiman; creep yourself out with Gergory Frost; laugh with Delia Sherman, and then read all the others.

Datlow, Ellen and Windling, Terri, Eds.
Teeth: Vampire Tales. 2011, HarperCollins, ISBN: 9780061935152, 452p.

Tired of fluffy vampire romances? Then try this anthology, filled with stories that reach back to old-time vampire lore. With offerings by authors such as Holly Black, Cassandra Clare, and Melissa Marr, readers will be sucked right into these sensual, dark, and sometimes scary stories.

November, Sharyn, Ed. ♛
Firebirds: An Anthology of Original Fantasy and Science Fiction. 2003, Firebird, ISBN: 9780142501429, 420p.

This collection offers stories from a wide variety of fantasy and sci-fi themes. Masters such as Diana Wynne Jones, Nancy Farmer, and Megan Whelan Turner offer retellings of fairy tales, changeling stories, beating evil in understated ways, and more. Whether you want to be scared out of your mind, taken to another world, or have a laugh, this collection has it all.

Strahan, Jonathan, Ed.
Life on Mars: Tales from the New Frontier: An Original Science Fiction Anthology. 2011, Viking, ISBN: 9780670012169, 400p.

Human imagination has always run wild around the topic of Mars, the planet closest to Earth in the solar system. What wonders might be contained on its red surface? Twelve top-notch science fiction authors (Ellen Klages,

Nancy Kress, etc.) answer that question and give us stories about a Mars that has been colonized.

Taylor, Lani ♈
Lips Touch: Three Times. 2009, Arthur A. Levine, ISBN: 9780545055857, 272p.
    A kiss can have amazing power, as each character in these three stories soon learn. High school junior Kizzy forgets everything she's learned about goblins when she falls under the spell of a handsome new student; Anamique is a girl in British-occupied India who has been cursed with silence and longs for love; Esme wakes up on her 14th birthday to discover that her body is hosting a nonhuman entity. Simply tasty.

Visual Language: Graphic Novels

Sometimes when you read, the pictures in your head are not enough—you want to literally see the story as it unfolds before you. That's when graphic novels come in. The following titles are some of the best in the last decade and appeal to a wide range of reading—and visual—tastes.

Asada, Hiroyuki ♈
▶ *Tegami Bachi. Letter Bee, Volume 1.* 2009, Viz/Shonen Jump, ISBN: 9781421529134, 189p.
    Gauche is a delivery boy, a letter bee, in the land of Amberground. Amberground is mostly a place of darkness, except for a man-made sun used almost exclusively by the elite class. Gauche is used to delivering letters on his mostly dark route, but one day he must deliver an orphan boy, Lan Seeing, who has just lost his mother.

Chmakova, Svetlana ♈
Nightschool: The Weirn Books. Nightschool, 1. 2009, Yen Press, ISBN: 9780759528598, 192p.
    Alex and her younger sister Sarah live in the mortal world but neither is human—they are *weirn* or witches. A past trauma keeps Alex from going to the Nightschool, where teen demons, vampires, and other *weirn* attend classes. Then Sarah disappears, and Alex is the only one who seems to remember her, so she must venture into the Nightschool to find out what happened.

Dekker, Ted; Illustrated by Caio Reis; Adapted by J. S. Earls
Chosen. Lost Books, 1. 2008, Thomas Nelson, ISBN: 9781595546036, 136p.
    Johnis is 16 and a reluctant participant of a quest with three other kids. To stop the decimation of the Forest Dwellers' land, Johnis and his companions must locate the seven missing Books of History that will give them power over the past, present, and future.

Iwahara, Yuji ♛
King of Thorn, Volume 1. 2007, Tokyopop, ISBN: 9781598162356, 161p.

The Medusa virus is a horrific disease that turns its victims into stone. One hundred and sixty people are selected to be cryogenically frozen until a cure is discovered. Kasumi is one of them, but she must leave behind her twin sister, Shizuku. When she is awakened from her frozen sleep, expecting all to be well, Kasumi finds a world ravaged by disease and monsters.

Shan, Darren ♛
Cirque du Freak. Cirque du Freak the Manga, 1. 2009, Yen Press, ISBN: 9780759530416, 186p.

Darren Shan is your average kid, walking home one night when he is handed a flyer to a circus. When Darren and his friend Steve get to the circus, however, they discover it is not your typical elephants-and-trapeze-act kind—it is filled with vampires, werewolves, and other freaks!

Siddel, Tom ♛
Gunnerkrigg Court, Volume 1: Orientation. 2008, Archaia Studios Press, ISBN: 9781932386349, 291p.

Antimony Carver attends a strange British boarding school called Gunnerkrigg Court, which is located across the river from an enchanted wood. Antimony is a reserved girl with perfect manners, but she learns to defend herself when she begins encountering shadow creatures, robots, Minotaurs, and more.

Whedon, Joss ♛
Fray. 2003, Dark Horse, ISBN: 9781569717516, 216p.

Melaka Fray lives as a street thief in a future Manhattan, grieving the loss of her twin brother and estranged from her sister. When a Watcher shows up and reveals she is a Slayer—a vampire hunter—she is not very excited, especially when it was vampires who killed her brother.

Willingham, Bill
Fables, Book 1: Legends in Exile. 2003, DC Comics, ISBN: 9781563899423, 128p.

In Fabletown, storybook characters live alongside their mortal New York counterparts. They are an unhappy lot, forced out of their Homelands by an adversary who has conquered their realm. When Snow White's sister, Rose Red, goes missing, it is the Wolf—now a reformed detective—who takes on the bloody case.

Moving Pictures: Comics into Movies

Chivalry is not dead and heroes really do exist in these awesome movies, born from comic book seeds. Sit back, relax, and watch your favorite good guys—or even your favorite love-to-hate-'em bad guys—come to life.

▶ **Batman Begins.** 2005, Warner Bros. Starring Christian Bale, Michael Caine. Directed by Christopher Nolan.

Gotham City is crime-ridden, and Bruce Wayne grows up watching his rich, philanthropist parents do their part to help the innocents. Years after Bruce's parents are murdered in a robbery, Bruce travels to the Far East to train in martial arts with Henri Ducard, a member of the mysterious League of Shadows. When he returns to Gotham City, Bruce has developed almost super-human senses and is determined to clean up the crime under the masked guise of Batman. Then a sadistic psychiatrist joins forces with powerful criminals, giving Batman a run for his money.

Captain America: The First Avenger. 2011, Marvel. Starring Chris Evans, Hugo Weaving. Directed by Joe Johnston.

Steve Rogers tries desperately to enlist in the army so he can fight in World War II, but his puny frame and asthma get in the way. Eventually his strong will lands him in the service, and a scientist takes an interest in him. After agreeing to participate in a chemical experiment, Steve Rogers transforms into Captain America—super strong with super speed—the country's best weapon. His arch nemesis? A breakaway Nazi named Schmidt, who has dosed himself with the chemical weapon to nightmarish proportions.

Hellboy. 2004, Columbia/Revolution. Starring Ron Perlman, Selma Blair. Directed by Guillermo Del Toro.

During World War II, the evil Rasputin has summoned a demon from Hades to use as the ultimate Axis weapon. When the creature is captured by American forces, it is turned over to Professor Broom, the founder of a top-secret U.S. organization. Professor Broom raises the creature, known as Hell-boy, to do good while still retaining his supernatural powers. When Hellboy is finally grown, he becomes part of an elite defense team with other supernatural beings, but his goodness is tested when Rasputin returns.

Iron Man. 2008, Paramount. Starring Robert Downey Jr., Terrence Howard. Directed by Jon Favreau.

Brilliant and filthy rich Tony Stark doesn't care about much. Then, when he is kidnapped in the Middle East, he uses his intelligence to build a suit of armor to escape his captors. Once home, Stark's philanthropy is awakened, and he continues to use the suit to benefit society. But soon he learns that a larger threat looms much closer to home than he would have imagined.

Spider Man. 2002, Columbia Pictures. Starring Tobey Maguire, Willem Dafoe. Directed by Sam Raimi.

Peter Parker is quiet and unassuming. He lives with his elderly aunt and uncle and dreams of Mary Jane, the beautiful girl next door. While on a field trip to a university lab, Peter is bitten by a genetically altered spider, and overnight he gains superhuman powers. At first, Peter can't believe his good luck; he uses his new talent for material gain—in fact, he sews up a red costume, calls himself Spider Man, and wins a wrestling match. But when tragedy strikes, Peter turns to fighting crime. Along the way, he gains a reputation—and a nemesis named the Green Goblin.

V for Vendetta. 2006, Warner Bros. Starring Natalie Portman, Hugo Weaving. Directed by James Mcteigue.

In an alternate version of Great Britain, the government is oppressive and totalitarian. Evey is a modest young woman who is attacked one night by secret police; a masked vigilante saves her; he calls himself V. The incident opens Evey's eyes, and she is drawn into V's plan to start a revolution.

X-Men. 2000, 20th Century Fox. Starring Hugh Jackman, Patrick Stewart. Directed by Bryan Singer.

Psychic professor Xavier runs a school for mutants called X-Men, where he provides training and a haven of sorts. His evil counterpart, Magneto, is a mutant with a powerful magnetic charge and has begun to organize a team to wipe out humanity. Both struggle for the loyalty of Wolverine, a rogue mutant with extreme strength and skill. On top of it all, an evil politician is leading a campaign that targets all mutants—and their extermination.

Language Comes Alive! Spec Lit on Audio

Listening to a novel has great advantages: it keeps you from strangling your annoying siblings on long car trips; it consoles you as you engage in boring household chores; it takes you away from the burn of running another mile in cross-country. Choose from any of these titles and prepare to be entertained in stereo.

Billingsley, Franny ♆

Chime. Read by Susan Duerden. 2011, Random House/Listening Library, ISBN: 9780307915214, 8 CDs.

Briony Larkin is a troubled 17-year-old, able to commune with the Old Ones of the Swampsea. Briony considers herself a witch, a curse that has destroyed her twin sister's mind and killed her stepmother. Things change when attractive new guy Eldric comes to town.

Card, Orson Scott

▶ *Ender's Game: Special 20th Anniversary Edition. Read by Stefan Rudnicki.* 2004, Audio Renaissance Audiobook, ISBN: 1593974744, 9 CDs.

In a future earth that has been battling alien invasion, young genius Ender is chosen to play what he believes to be a computer war game. In truth, Ender and his abilities are being used to wipe out the alien race entirely.

Colfer, Eoin ♆

Artemis Fowl 4: Opal Deception. Read by Nathaniel Parker. 2005, Random House/Listening Library, ISBN: 0307243338, 6 CDs.

Criminal mastermind Artemis Fowl is now 14, and his mind has been completely wiped clean of all fairy knowledge—and all of the goodness he has finally learned. This is good news for fairy (and arch nemesis of Artemis) Opal Koboi, who has plans to destroy the world.

Cooper, Susan 🏆
Over Sea, Under Stone. The Dark Is Rising Sequence, Book One. Read by Alex Jennings. 2007, Listening Library, ISBN: 9780739361962, 6 CDs.

While on summer vacation at the Grey House in Cornwall, siblings Simon, Jane, and Barney find an old map. Soon they are embroiled in a dangerous quest for the holy grail of King Arthur lore.

Enthoven, Sam 🏆
The Black Tattoo. Read by John Lee. 2006, Random House/Listening Library, ISBN: 0739337815, 11 CDs.

Jack lives in London, has always been a follower, and is kind of bored. Then his best friend, Charlie, gets possessed by an ancient evil called the Scourge, who leaves the mark of a writhing tattoo. Determined to be a leader in his friend's rescue, Jack and a young martial arts expert, Esme, chase Charlie all over London (and even into Hell) to save him.

Roth, Veronica 🏆
Divergent. Read by Emma Galvin. 2011, Harper Audio, ISBN: 9780062095909, 11 CDs.

In a future, decimated Chicago, people are divided into five factions—Abnegation, Candor, Dauntless, Erudite, and Amity—depending on their beliefs. A person must choose the faction where they will work and reside forever when they reach age 16, forbidden to make contact with anyone they leave behind—including families. Tris feels she must stay with her Abnegation faction for the sake of her parents, but surprises everyone when she chooses to be a Dauntless.

Rowling, J. K. 🏆
Harry Potter and the Deathly Hallows. Read by Jim Dale. 2007, Random House/Listening Library, ISBN: 9780739360385, 17 CDs.

Harry, Ron, and Hermione set out on the seemingly impossible task of locating the rest of the Horcruxes, where Voldemort has stored pieces of his soul, in an effort to stop the Dark Lord's invasion. Harry must use all of his skills and lessons from the past six years to complete this, his final task.

Faster Than a Speeding Bullet! Short, Quick Reads

Not sure if you like spec lit? Just looking for a taste? Or maybe you've got an hour to kill on the plane, the train, or the submarine. Grab any of these short but sweet titles, and I guarantee you'll want more.

Forman, Gail 🏆
If I Stay. 2009, Dutton Books, ISBN: 9780525421030, 199p.

Seventeen-year-old Mia, a gifted cellist with college plans at Julliard, lies in a coma after a devastating car wreck kills the rest of her family. She is wrenched from her body and is able to watch herself and reflect on her life—her friends, boyfriend, future. Over the next 24 hours, Mia will need to decide to fight for her life, or to go into the unknown with her family.

Gray, Amy
How to Be a Vampire: A Fangs-On Guide for the Newly Undead. 2010, Candlewick Press, ISBN: 9780763649159, 144p.

If you are a newly made vampire, then this guide is for you. Filled with useful information such as "Leaving the Mortal Realm" and "Living the Undead Lifestyle," this handbook makes transitioning into a bloodsucker a cinch.

Holt, K. A.
Brains for Lunch: A Zombie Novel in Haiku. 2010, Roaring Brook Press, ISBN: 9781596436299, 96p.

Middle school is rough, but imagine sitting next to a zombie or a *chupacabra* in algebra. This is the story of Loeb, a zombie, who nurses a crush on a Lifer (a human girl) and tries his hand at open-mike poetry. Told in haiku form, this is a pretty cool book; share it with your friends.

Myers, Walter Dean
▶ *Dope Sick.* 2009, HarperTeen/Amistad, ISBN: 9780061214783, 192p.

Seventeen-year-old Lil J lives in Harlem and has made a lot of mistakes, the latest a drug deal gone wrong and an undercover cop shot. Lil J takes refuge in an abandoned building as the cops gather in the street, and he frantically searches for a way out. A vagrant in the building invites LiL J to watch his special TV, view scenes from his life, and contemplate what he might change if given the chance.

Viguie, Debbie
Midnight Pearls. Once Upon a Time. 2003, Simon Pulse, ISBN: 9780689855573, 197p.

A fisherman finds a girl floating in the sea, clutching a large blue pearl, and he takes her home to his wife. The couple raises the child, who turns out to be long, extremely thin, and pale. Her only friend is the prince, and the two have been meeting on the beach weekly. They are on the verge of romance when vengeful mermaids get involved.

Worley, Rob M.
Heir to Fire: Gila Flats. 2006, Actionopolis, ISBN: 9780974280370, 129p.

Fourteen-year-old Ryan has always been warm-blooded—ice cream melts in his hands and fires seem to ignite whenever he is around. Soon he uncovers the truth—his parents found him as an infant, abandoned in the desert; Ryan is actually from another planet and is the Fire Prince. When he opens a portal, horrific monsters and an even deeper evil are unleashed, and he must find a way to use his birthright to save his family.

Let Me Tell You Something: First-Person Narratives

Occasionally when you read, you'd like to feel close to the main character—so close, in fact, that you want to be right inside her head. Well, you can't get much closer than these first-person narratives—live the magic through these characters' very eyes!

Banner, Catherine
The Eyes of a King. Last Descendants Trilogy, 1. 2008, Random House Children's Books, ISBN: 9780375838750, 435p.

Fifteen-year-old Leo lives in war-torn Maloria, where the government is corrupt and all young men will eventually join the army. He finds respite in a magical book that writes stories about a mythical land called England. As Leo reads more of the story, he begins to suspect that the true prince of Maloria is not really dead but has been banished to this land. So begins a journey into parallel universes.

Gratton, Tessa
Blood Magic. 2011, Random House Children's Books, ISBN: 9780375867330, 408p.

Silla is a disturbed teen living in Missouri. Her parents allegedly committed a murder-suicide, but she's not so sure. When a mysterious book arrives in the mail, Silla discovers that it's filled with spells, all requiring the ingredient of blood. Enter Nick, who is drawn to Silla by his own grief. Together they decide to try a few of the blood spells, hoping to uncover the truth.

Hardy, Janice
The Shifter. Healing Wars, 1. 2009, Balzer & Bray, ISBN: 9780061747045, 370p.

Nya and her younger sister Tali are orphans living in a war-torn city. Both girls are shifters—able to shift pain out of people and into something else. Tali can shift the pain into an enchanted metal storage compartment and is therefore valuable to the Healer's League. Nya, however, can only shift pain onto herself or others and is therefore not valued. She keeps her powers hidden and scrounges out a life for herself until a young soldier uncovers her secret and begs for her help. Then she must make a choice.

Kogler, Jennifer Anne
The Death Catchers. 2011, Walker Books for Young Readers, ISBN: 9780802721846, 352p.

Lizzy is an average 14-year-old living in Crabapple, California—at least she thinks she's average until she begins to see death specters. Soon Lizzy learns that both she and her grandmother are descended from the mystical Morgan le Fay and can foresee the deaths of others. This leads Lizzy to grapple with the question, if she can see the future, might she be able to change it?

McKinley, Robin
▶ *Dragonhaven.* 2007, G. P. Putnam's Sons, ISBN: 9780399246753, 272p.
Jake has grown up in Smokehill National Park, a reserve where dragons are federally protected. When he goes on his first solo expedition, he finds a newborn dragon whose mother has been killed by poachers and tries to raise the creature himself. There's only one problem—saving a dragon and removing it from the wild is illegal.

Schwab, Victoria
The Near Witch. 2011, Hyperion Books, ISBN: 9781423137870, 288p.
Sixteen-year-old Lexi has heard the legend of the Near Witch all her life, and in fact believes in witches. She visits the witch sisters, an elderly pair of women, who live on the outskirts of their isolated village. When children begin to disappear, the villagers blame a young man who has mysteriously appeared—but Lexi is not so quick to judge. She and the young man, Cole, work to uncover the mystery and to find the missing children.

Whitman, Emily
Wildwing. 2010, Greenwillow Books, ISBN: 9780061724527, 359p.
In 1913 London, 15-year-old Addy wants nothing more than to continue her schooling and to rise above her station. This is not to be and she is employed as a house servant to a strange, depressed hermit of a man. In her free time, Addy explores the drafty old house, gets inside an elevator, and is somehow transported to the year 1240—where she becomes the intended bride for a rich man.

Wood, Maryrose
The Poison Diaries. 2010, Balzer & Bray, ISBN: 9780061802362, 278p.
In 18th century England, 16-year-old Jessamine lives with her father, who is the local apothecary. Her father keeps a locked garden in which he grows poisonous plants from all over the world; she is forbidden to ever enter this garden. Then a young man named Weed shows up. He demonstrates an almost magical quality for growing plants, and as romance heats up between him and Jessamine, she allows him into her father's garden. The results are disastrous for everyone.

Challenge Yourself! Adult/Teen Crossovers

Maybe you're on summer break and have more time to delve into a huge fantasy tome. Or perhaps the snow is deep, the wind is cold, and you just want to curl up in front of the fire with some multilayered fiction. These crossover novels may be more involved than others, but you can handle it!

Briggs, Patricia
Moon Called. Mercy Thompson Series, 1. 2006, Ace Books, ISBN: 9780441013814, 288p.

Mercy Thompson, a skinwalker, was given up by her mother and raised in a werewolf clan. Knowing she has always been an outcast, she tries to live a quiet life running a garage, but she has a vampire neighbor to one side, an Alpha werewolf on the other, and quiet is hardly an option. When an injured teen comes to her door, Mercy uncovers a strange plot involving werewolf experimentation.

Brooks, Terry
Armageddon's Children. Genesis of Shannara, 1. 2006, Del Ray, ISBN: 9780345484086, 384p.

In a futuristic world, the United States has fallen to ruin, and entire populations have been wiped out due to disease, global warming, and war. With mutated creatures roaming the streets, remaining humans hide out in stadiums and other fortresses. Logan Tom and his friend Angel Peres are Knights of the Word, committed to keeping magic safe, and they set out to find a mythical child who may hold the magic to save the world.

Butcher, Jim
Storm Front. Dresden Files, 1. 2000, ROC, ISBN: 9780451457813, 322p.

Meet Harry Dresden, a mage who works with the Chicago police to solve a bloody double homicide that appears to have been committed by black magic. The deeper Harry gets involved, the more he realizes that is was black magic used in the crime—and a rival dark mage is behind it.

Gaiman, Neil ♈
Anansi Boys. 2005, William Morrow, ISBN: 9780060515188, 368p.

Fat Charlie has been living an uneventful life in London when he discovers his estranged—and extremely embarrassing father—has died. After returning home to Florida for the funeral, Charlie meets the brother he'd never known, who is named Spider, and learns that his father was actually Anansi, the West African trickster god. Spider soon starts to work his own magic on Charlie, getting him fired, stealing his girlfriend, and so on, until Charlie decides to fight back.

Harris, Charlaine
Dead until Dark. Sookie Stackhouse Novels, 1. 2001, Ace Books, ISBN: 9780441008537, 260p.

Vampires have come out and are attempting to join human society. Sookie Stackhouse is a waitress in a small Louisiana bar and can read minds, an ability that has pretty much been a torture her entire life. When Vampire Bill comes in one night, Sookie discovers she can't read his thoughts, something that is so intriguing to her that they begin to date. But messing around with vampires will always come back to bite you—when one of Sookie's coworkers is murdered, everyone suspects Vampire Bill.

King, Stephen
The Gunslinger. Dark Tower, 1. 2003, Viking, ISBN: 9780670032549, 315p.

In this futuristic Western where the landscape is dead, Roland is the last gunslinger and is on a quest to learn the secrets of the Dark Tower. Roland and his friends find themselves tracking the Man in Black through the Waste Lands because Roland believes the man is the key to answering all his questions.

Rothfuss, Patrick ♛
▶ *The Name of the Wind. Kingkiller Chronicles, 1.* 2007, DAW, ISBN: 9780756404079, 896p.

A bard uncovers the identity of Kvothe, a legendary hero who is now hiding out as an innkeeper under a different name. When the bard begs Kvothe to tell his story, Kvothe does, giving voice to his long, winding path from boy to young man to wizard. All the while, evil creatures are roaming about who may or may not be attracted to the legendary figure.

Tolkien, J.R.R.
The Tale of the Children of Hurin. 2007, Houghton Mifflin, ISBN: 9780618894642, 313p.

In a pre-Hobbit Middle Earth, Lord Hurin is battling the Dark Lord Morgoth; his elven wife, Lady Morwen, fears for their son Turin's safety, so she sends him to live in Doriath. Years later, Turin is wrongly accused of murdering an elf and is banished from Doriath. He joins up with a ragtag band of outlaws, who decide to take part in the fight against the Dark Lord and his minions— Orcs, dragons, and more. But an old curse is at play, and Turin may be doomed.

From the Masters: Epic Fantasy and Sci-Fi

The titles in this list contain everything you love about fantasy and speculative fiction—they've just been around longer. Think of them as blueprints for all of the amazing fiction that has come after. Here you will find epic quests, richly imagined worlds, intense relationships between characters, and the continual battle of good versus evil.

Bradley, Marion Zimmer ♛
The Mists of Avalon. Avalon Series. 7. 2000, Ballantine Books, ISBN: 9780345441188, 876p.

This is the novel that retells Arthurian legend from the point of view of the women. Morgaine is the priestess of Avalon, able to move her spirit in and out of the mysterious mists of Avalon (another dimension). Morgaine represents the pagan ways and is uncomfortable with the new Christian religion taking over Briton. She supports her half-brother Arthur on Camelot's throne with magic and the sword Excalibur, but the tension increases when Arthur's wife, Gwenhwyfar, becomes more and more obsessed with Christianity.

Brooks, Terry
The Sword of Shannara. Sword of Shannara Trilogy, 1. 1977, Ballantine Books, ISBN: 9780345248046, 726p.

Shea is a half-elven child raised in Shady Vale by a family who runs an inn. The family's son, Flick, and Shea bond as closely as brothers. What Shea does not know is that he is the last descendant of the Sword of Shannara, the only weapon capable of defeating the Warlock Lord—who has risen again. Circumstances force Shea, Flick, and a group of friends made up of two elves, a prince, and a dwarf on a search for the sword.

Herbert, Frank ♈
Dune. Dune Novels, Main Series, 1. 1984, G. P. Putnam's Sons, ISBN: 9780399128967, 517p.

Ten thousand years in the future, the world's most coveted export, Melange—an addictive substance nicknamed "spice"—is mined only from the desert sands on the planet Arrakis. Two powerful families jockey for control of the spice—the Harkonnen Noble House and the House Atreides. Young Paul Atreides is the heir apparent and through political treachery, he is cast out into the desert to presumably die, but Paul proves he's got resilience—in fact, he might even be the Messiah.

Jordan, Robert
The Eye of the World. The Wheel of Time, 1. 1990, TOR, ISBN: 9780312850098, 670p.

Without warning, the peaceful community of Emond's Field is attacked by Trollocs—violent creatures who serve the Evil One. Three young men, Rand, Perrin, and Mat, are the targets of the attack; to save their people, the young men flee. The friends are relentlessly pursued, and as they struggle to understand the situation, they move closer to the Eye of the World, the only thing the Evil One fears, because it can destroy him.

Kay, Guy Gavriel
The Summer Tree. Fionavar Tapestry, 1. 2001, ROC, ISBN: 9780451458223, 383p.

After attending a lecture by an odd professor, five university students—Kimberly, Dave, Jennifer, Kevin, and Paul—learn that he is really Loren Silvercloak, a mage from Fionavar—the heart of all worlds. He invites the friends back with him to celebrate the 50th year of the reign of their king. The five agree, and once they reach Fionavar, they discover wonderful and horrible things, about themselves and the magical land.

Martin, George R. R. ♛

A Game of Thrones. Song of Fire and Ice, 1. 1996, Bantam Books, ISBN: 9780553103540, 694p.

In the Seven Kingdoms, climate change has wrought decades-long seasons and a draining of magic. Three powerful families once came together to depose their insane king. Robert claimed the throne while Ned Stark returned home to the north. Years later, with his kingdom unraveling, Robert asks Ned to come south and help govern. What follows is political deceit, treachery, magic, and lots and lots of violence.

Tolkien, J.R.R.

▶ *The Fellowship of the Ring. Lord of the Rings, 1.* 2001, Houghton Mifflin, ISBN: 9780618153985, 423p.

Originally published in 1954, Tolkien's trilogy is probably one of the most familiar in the fantasy world. Frodo the hobbit and his companions set out to deliver the One Ring of Power to the dark land of Mordor in order to destroy it and all evil.

Awards

Alex Awards

2008 Patrick Rothfuss   *The Name of the Wind: Kingkiller Chronicles, 1*
2006 Neil Gaiman   *Anansi Boys*

ALA Notable Children's Books—Older Readers Category

2011 Paul Bacigalupi   *Ship Breaker*
2010 Scott Westerfeld   *Leviathan*
2009 Suzanne Collins   *The Hunger Games*
2008 Kate Thompson   *The New Policeman*
2006 Shannon Hale   *Princess Academy*
      Rick Riordan   *The Lightning Thief: Percy Jackson and the Olympians, 1*
      Gabrielle Zevin   *Elsewhere*
2005 Nancy Farmer   *Sea of Trolls: Sea of Trolls Trilogy, 1*
      Catherine Fisher   *The Oracle Betrayed: Oracle Prophecies, 1*
      Michael Gruber   *The Witch's Boy*
      Kenneth Opel   *Airborn*

2004	Cornelia Funke	*Inkheart*
	Edith Pattou	*East*
	Terry Pratchett	*The Wee Free Men*
	Phillip Reeve	*Mortal Engines*
	Jonathan Stroud	*Amulet of Samarkand: Bartimaeus Trilogy 1*
2003	Nancy Farmer	*The House of the Scorpion*
	Neil Gaiman	*Coraline*
2002	David Almond	*Heaven Eyes*
	Kevin Holland-Crossley	*The Seeing-Stone*
	Peter Dickinson	*The Ropemaker*
2001	J. K. Rowling	*Harry Potter and the Goblet of Fire*
1999	J. K. Rowling	*Harry Potter and the Sorcerer's Stone*
1997	Garth Nix	*Sabriel: Abhorsen Trilogy, 1*
	Philip Pullman	*The Golden Compass: His Dark Materials, 1*

Edgar Allen Poe Awards: Best Juvenile Mystery Novel

| 2008 | Katherine Marsh | *The Night Tourist* |

Hugo Awards

2009	Neil Gaiman	*The Graveyard Book*
2001	J. K. Rowling	*Harry Potter and the Goblet of Fire*
1966	Frank Herbert	*Dune*

Locus Awards: Fantasy Novel

2009	Kristin Cashore	*Graceling*
2007	Catherine Fisher	*Corbenic*
	J. K. Rowling	*Harry Potter and the Deathly Hallows*
2006	Justine Larbalestier	*Magic or Madness*
	Jonathan Stroud	*Bartimaeus Trilogy*
2004	Clare B. Dunkle	*The Hollow Kingdom*

2003	Michael Chabon	*Summerland*
2002	Peter Dickinson	*The Ropemaker*
1997	George R. R. Martin	*A Game of Thrones*
1984	Marion Zimmer Bradley	*The Mists of Avalon*
1966	Frank Herbert	*Dune*

Locus Awards: Young Adult Book Award

2011	Paul Bacigalupi	*Ship Breaker*
2010	Scott Westerfeld	*Leviathan*
2009	Neil Gaiman	*The Graveyard Book*
2006	Jane Yolen	*Pay the Piper: A Rock n' Roll Fairy Tale*

Michael L. Printz Award

| 2011 | Paul Bacigalupi | *Ship Breaker* |

Newbery Award

| 2009 | Neil Gaiman | *The Graveyard Book* |

YALSA Best Books for Young Adults

2011	Paul Bacigalupi	*Ship Breaker*
	Holly Black	*The White Cat*
	Elizabeth C. Bunce	*Starcrossed*
	Frank Boyce Cottrell	*Cosmic*
	James Dashner	*The Maze Runner*
	Catherine Fisher	*Incarceron*
	Allyson Braithwaite Condie	*Matched*
	Melina Marchetta	*Finnikin of the Rock*
	Caragh O'Brien	*Birthmarked*
	Polly Shulman	*The Grimm Legacy*
	Sharon Shinn	*Gateway*

2011 Arthur Slade   *The Hunchback Assignments*
      Andrew Smith   *The Marbury Lens*
      Heather Tomlinson   *Toads and Diamonds*
      Rachel Ward   *Num8ers*
      Brenna Yovanoff   *The Replacement*
2010 Sarah Ree Brennan   *The Demon's Lexicon*
      Kristin Cashore   *Fire: Graceling Prequel*
      Gail Forman   *If I Stay*
      Jessica Day George   *Princess of the Midnight Ball*
      David Macinnis Gill   *Soul Enchilada*
      Alison Goodman   *Eon: Dragoneye Reborn*
      Carrie Ryan   *The Forest of Hands and Teeth*
      Maggie Stiefvater   *Lament: The Faerie Queen's Deception*
      Maggie Stiefvater   *Shiver: Wolves of Mercy Falls, 1*
      Lani Taylor   *Lips Touch: Three Times*
      Scott Westerfeld   *Leviathan*
      Rick Yancy   *The Monstrumologist*
2009 Elizabeth C. Bunce   *A Curse Dark as Gold*
      Kristin Cashore   *Graceling*
      Eoin Colfer   *Airman*
      Suzanne Collins   *The Hunger Games*
      Cory Doctorow   *Little Brother*
      Neil Gaiman   *The Graveyard Book*
      Jessica Day George   *Sun and Moon, Ice and Snow*
      Graham McNamee   *Bonechiller*
      Patrick Ness   *The Knife of Never Letting Go*
      Mary Pearson   *The Adoration of Jenna Fox*
2008 Shannon Hale   *Book of a Thousand Days*
      David Klass   *Firestorm: Caretaker Trilogy, 1*
      Juliet Marillier   *Wildwood Dancing*
      Marcus Sedgwick   *My Swordhand Is Singing*
      Neal Shusterman   *Unwind*
      Kate Thompson   *The New Policeman*
2007 D. M. Cornish   *Foundling: Monster Blood Tattoo, 1*
      Maureen Johnson   *Devilish*
      Susan Beth Pfeffer   *Life as We Knew It*
      Tamora Pierce   *Terrier: Beka Cooper*
2006 L. J. Adlington   *The Diary of Pelly D*
      Joseph Delaney   *Revenge of the Witch: Last Apprentice, 1*
      Neil Gaiman   *Anansi Boys*
      Michael Gruber   *The Witch's Boy*
      Julie Hearn   *The Minister's Daughter*
      Justine Larbalestier   *Magic or Madness*

	Stephanie Meyer	*Twilight*
	Rick Riordan	*The Lightning Thief: Percy Jackson and the Olympians, 1*
	Scott Westerfeld	*Peeps*
	Laura Whitcomb	*A Certain Slant of Light*
2005	Charles de Lint	*The Blue Girl*
	Nancy Farmer	*Sea of Trolls: Sea of Trolls Trilogy, 1*
	Catherine Fisher	*The Oracle Betrayed: Oracle Prophecies, 1*
	Kenneth Opel	*Airborn*
	Chris Wooding	*The Haunting of Alaizabel Cray*
2004	Hilari Bell	*The Goblin Wood*
	Herbie Brennan	*Faerie Wars*
	Sharyn November	*Firebirds: An Anthology of Original Fantasy and Science Fiction*
	Edith Pattou	*East*
	Terry Pratchett	*The Wee Free Men*
	Phillip Reeve	*Mortal Engines*
	Jonathan Stroud	*Amulet of Samarkand: Bartimaeus Trilogy, 1*
	Jane Yolen	*Sword of the Rightful King: A Novel of King Arthur*
2003	M. T. Anderson	*Feed*
	Andrew Clements	*Things Not Seen*
	Nancy Farmer	*The House of the Scorpion*
	Neil Gaiman	*Coraline*
	Ann Halam	*Dr. Franklin's Island*
	Sherryl Jordan	*The Hunting of the Last Dragon*
2002	Celia Rees	*Witch Child*
	Meredith Ann Pierce	*Treasure at the Heart of Tanglewood*
	Terry Pratchett	*The Amazing Maurice and His Educated Rodents*
2001	Mary Logue	*Dancing with an Alien*
1998	Annette Curtis Klause	*Blood and Chocolate*
1997	Garth Nix	*Sabriel: Abhorsen Trilogy, 1*
	Philip Pullman	*The Golden Compass: His Dark Materials, 1*
1996	Vivian Vande Velde	*Companions of the Night*

YALSA Great Graphic Novels for Teens

2010	Hiroyuki Asada	*Tegami Bachi: Letter Bee, Volume 1*
	Svetlana Chmakova	*Nightschool: The Weirn Books*
	Darren Shan	*Cirque du Freak the Manga 1*

2010 Tom Siddel   *Gunnerkrigg Court, Volume 1: Orientation*
2008 Yuji Iwahara   *King of Thorn, Volume 1*
2005 Joss Whedon   *Fray*

YALSA 100 Best Books (1950–2000)

1999 Francesca Lia Block   *Weetzie Bat*

Appendix Two

Audio Awards

ALSC Notable Children's Recordings

2008 *Harry Potter and the Deathly Hallows*
    Written by J. K. Rowling; Read by Jim Dale
2006 *Artemis Fowl 4: Opal Deception*
    Written by Eoin Colfer; Read by Nathanial Parker
2002 *Over Sea, Under Stone. The Dark Is Rising Sequence, Book One*
    Written by Susan Cooper; Read by Alex Jennings

Audie Awards

2008 *Harry Potter and the Deathly Hallows*
    Written by J. K. Rowling; Read by Jim Dale

AudioFile Earphones Award Winner

2011 *Chime*
    Written by Franny Billingsley; Read by Susan Duerden
    Divergent
    Written by Veronica Roth; Read by Emma Galvin

2007 *Harry Potter and the Deathly Hallows*
Written by J. K. Rowling; Read by Jim Dale

GRAMMY Awards (Best Spoken Word for Children)

2008 *Harry Potter and the Deathly Hallows*
Written by J. K. Rowling; Read by Jim Dale

Odyssey Award

2008 *Harry Potter and the Deathly Hallows*
Written by J. K. Rowling; Read by Jim Dale

YALSA Amazing Audiobooks for Young Adults

2008 *The Black Tattoo*
Written by Sam Enthoven; Read by John Lee
2008 *Harry Potter and the Deathly Hallows*
Written by J. K. Rowling; Read by Jim Dale

Index

115

About the Author

JAMIE KALLIO works as a Youth Services librarian at Orland Park Public Library in Illinois and has long been a writer. She first discovered fantasy fiction with *The Lion, the Witch, and the Wardrobe* in the third grade. Ever since, she has been climbing into wardrobes looking for a magical snowy land.